Barry Crump wrote his first bo⟨...⟩ *Good Keen Man*, in 1960. It became a ⟨...⟩ s did his numerous other books ⟨...⟩ s most famous and best-love⟨...⟩ Sam Cash, who feat⟨...⟩ *Mate*, Crump's se⟨...⟩ ⟨...⟩ese two books have sc⟨...⟩ ⟨...⟩d continue to sell at an amazi⟨...⟩ ⟨...⟩rs later.

Crump began his ⟨...⟩g life as a professional hunter, culling deer and pigs in some of the ruggedest country in New Zealand. After the runaway success of his first book, he pursued many diverse activities, including goldmining, radio talkback, white-baiting, television presenting, crocodile shooting and acting.

As to classifying his occupation, Crump always insisted that he was a Kiwi bushman.

He published 25 books and was awarded the MBE for services to literature in 1994.

Books by Barry Crump

A Good Keen Man (1960)
Hang on a Minute Mate (1961)
One of Us (1962)
There and Back (1963)
Gulf (1964) – now titled *Crocodile Country*
Scrapwaggon (1965)
The Odd Spot of Bother (1967)
No Reference Intended (1968)
Warm Beer and Other Stories (1969)
A Good Keen Girl (1970)
Bastards I Have Met (1970)
Fred (1972)
Shorty (1980)
Puha Road (1982)
The Adventures of Sam Cash (1985)
Wild Pork and Watercress (1986)
Barry Crump's Bedtime Yarns (1988)
Bullock Creek (1989)
The Life and Times of a Good Keen Man (1992)
Gold and Greenstone (1993)
Arty and the Fox (1994)
Forty Yarns and a Song (1995)
Mrs Windyflax and the Pungapeople (1995)
Crumpy's Campfire Companion (1996)
As the Saying Goes (1996)
A Tribute to Crumpy: Barry Crump 1935–1996 is an anthology of tributes, extracts from Crump's books, letters and pictures from his private photo collection.

All titles currently (1997) in print.

CROCODILE
COUNTRY
(GULF)

BARRY CRUMP

CROCODILE COUNTRY (GULF)

Illustrated by Will Mahony

Hodder Moa Beckett

First edition (Gulf) 1964
Reprints numerous
This edition (Crocodile Country) 1994
Reprinted 1997

ISBN 1-86958-577-1

© 1964 Barry Crump

Published by Hodder Moa Beckett Publishers Limited
[a member of the Hodder Headline Group]
4 Whetu Place, Mairangi Bay, Auckland, New Zealand

Printed by McPherson's Printing Group, Australia

Cover Photo: NZPL/Leo Meier

Contents

Chapter		Page
1	A Complete Shambles	11
2	Best Croc-shooters in Queensland	23
3	An Ordinary Looking Bloke	37
4	Pruszkowic	55
5	The Yaloginda Pub	71
6	Crocs and Stuffers	91
7	Big Salty	109
8	Around the Gulf	129
9	Goodbye to Yaloginda	149
10	A Dinghy Like Darcy's	165
11	With Darcy Again	177
12	Most of the Time	191

Yaloginda is a fictitious town on the banks of the fictitious Manara River in the Gulf of Carpentaria. The Cleland River is fictitious too, as are the characters and dogs in this book – but if anyone can tell me where I can get a dog like Pruszkowic I'd be please to hear from them.

1

A Complete Shambles

THE OLD DRAGON came in from the kitchen with cups of tea. She sat on the floor, fair between me and the heater.

"A flaming joker wouldn't like to change his shirt would he?" she said. "You've been wearing that one for three days now and I've just put clean sheets on the bed."

"Shut up. I'm thinking. And don't call me a flaming joker."

I'm always having to pull her into gear over giving cheek like that.

"My big fierce bushman doesn't like taking his shirt off in the cold weather, does he?" she went on. "What would you like for your lunch tomorrow? There's cold meat, or tomato and onion."

"Nothing. I'm not going back there. Told the boss exactly what he could do with his forklift. The only time I would have liked that crawling topper of a foreman to be there he had to be away getting his buck teeth out. I had some advice ready for him, but it's wasted now. Anyway a man's finished with the blasted outfit. Don't know how I stuck it out as long as I did."

"Oh good. Now we can go 'roo-shooting again." She didn't seem to be very upset about me throwing in the factory job.

"Damn the 'roos," I said yawning. But she either didn't hear properly or she didn't believe it.

She took the empty cups into the kitchen. I stood up and got my coat off the back of the chair.

"Think I'll nick down to the pub for a while," I said. She didn't say anything so I said it louder. She should have been kicking up a stink about me promising we'd have an early night and read in bed.

She came and dragged my best jacket off me with the wet dishcloth still in her hand, saying: "You're not going to any pub and that's flat! With a new place for us to go not even talked about. It's your turn to go to bed first and warm the sheets."

Four months in town hadn't done the old dragon much good, I thought to myself. She was getting cheekier than ever. It was about time a joker showed her who was boss of this outfit.

When we were settled properly in bed I told her how I might just be thinking of going crocodile-shooting in the Gulf of Carpentaria. Then I pretended to go to sleep while she was still full of excitement and questions — but I started grinning and ruined it. The way she went on you'd think I'd jacked the whole thing up as a surprise especially for her. If she wanted to think that, I couldn't stop her. But it's not true all the same.

It was a bit of a surprise to me, as a matter of fact. I got the idea from an article in a magazine I was looking through at smoko that morning, and I'd thrown in the job that afternoon.

Fiff churned around in the bed for a while, letting cold air in all over the place and asking stupid questions. Then she ploughed right across my stomach with bony elbows and knees and skipped out of the room to get something to write on. They can hurt a man doing that. You don't know whether to watch out for an elbow in the eye or a knee somewhere else. They don't seem to realise. Makes a joker nervous.

She got back in with her exercise-book diary and wrote out a list of things to be done, and another of things to be taken, which included everything we had and quite a lot that had to be got. Then she drew up an agreement making me promise to leave all the packing and loading of our things into the Landrover entirely to her, except for my rifles, which were to be put behind the front seats wrapped in the grey blanket with the burn in it. Burnt side out. There was a no-growling-or-rushing-her clause, in case she got flustered and forgot things. And another saying I wasn't to go further away than the pub on the corner without telling her, in case she wanted me to carry things — there were two pages of it. I checked it through for mistakes, wrote in an expiry date and signed it.

Fiff witnessed my signature and wrote in a space above it that the penalty for breaking the agreement was no something-or-other till we got to the Gulf of Carpentaria. No comment.

A man couldn't help laughing. It was only four

months since we'd shifted last. We were moving around all the time but whenever we loaded the Landrover there was a great performance. Mainly because of all the junk she accumulated and wouldn't part with. One of these days I'm going to have a real clean-up but I haven't got around to it yet.

Anyway she hadn't even been officially invited on this trip. This croc-shooting was supposed to be a pretty dangerous game. A man wouldn't want to be tearing round all the time seeing that she didn't get into trouble. I was thinking of leaving her in Sydney till I'd had a look if it was suitable for a woman up there. I'd even wondered about jacking up a mate to go with me. But the only blokes I knew in Sydney who'd be any good were tied up with women or down with jobs, and they probably couldn't get away or weren't trying to. If I was going to leave within the next couple of days it wouldn't give anyone enough time to get ready anyway — might even get in with an experienced bloke up there somewhere.

I had just about everything I needed to kick off croc-shooting with, as far as I could make out, and a few quid to keep me going till I picked up a few clues about the game. I could afford to have a look round when I got up north and find out what kind of boats they used, and where the best places were. I had rifles and camping-gear and spotlights and things — stuff I'd been using on the 'roo-shooting last year, and what I didn't have now I could get later.

I should never have signed that agreement. The day we left Sydney was a complete shambles. She had our stuff scattered all over the footpath for hours, in full view of everybody, while she put things in the

Landrover and then took them out again because it wasn't quite right, or it might get broken there. And she kept calling out to people we hardly knew that we were going on a long journey to be crocodile-shooters. When I couldn't stand it any longer I went along to the pub and hid out in the private bar.

I didn't go back till I was absolutely certain she'd have everything loaded and be waiting for me to do the canopy up, but there was still stuff scattered on the footpath when I looked around the corner. She was taking things out of one box and putting them in another, as far as I could make out, and holding something up to show to a few people who were standing there.

I went back to the pub and stayed till she looked in the door and called out through the bar that we were all ready to set off for the Gulf of Carpentaria to go crocodile-shooting. I'm never going back to that place again.

It was after eleven-thirty when we finally got away. The cab of the Landrover was crammed with so much junk there was hardly room to move. Everything we might need in a hurry, from a snake-bite kit to a tin for putting brake-fluid in the master-cylinder. There were road maps for the whole of Australia and New Guinea and the exercise-book diary for writing down things that happened. Rags for the windscreen, rugs for our knees and a bottle of orange cordial so we wouldn't have to stop at pubs when I got thirsty. My seat felt a bit uncomfortable after a while so when I stopped at a pub two hours out of Sydney I had a look and found the big thick mat off the front porch rolled up behind my seat, preventing it from leaning back properly. She'd nearly left it behind, she reckoned, but I didn't forget to.

The first part of the trip was the worst. We had a hell of a row about her mucking up getting away. She said there was a special way of loading vehicles like ours because of the shape of the inside of the back and everything had to be sorted out in its right order. And she'd simply had to telephone her parents in Adelaide to tell them about us going to be crocodile-shooters. I hadn't forgotten about us having to get married in the registry office in Perth because of her old man, and now she goes and spends three quid on a toll-call to tell them where to send their stupid birthday cards that had been arriving too late the last year or so. She reckoned they'd forgiven us and that was their way of showing us, but I couldn't care less. She liked to get their little notes though. I suppose a joker was a bit unreasonable. I think I blamed her for getting crook so we had to go and live in Sydney in the first place. Ah well. That didn't worry her as much as me not letting her look after our travellers' cheques and money.

Once we got really clear of the towns I forgot to be angry with her. It was good to be away from Sydney and going somewhere again. We ended up yelling for each other to look at things and played our old game of seeing who was first to say "There's one!" when there was a kangaroo or emu. She was wearing the brown dress she had on when I first called her Fiffy. It made her look like a leaf.

After that the longest quarrel we had was between Cunnamulla and Coongoola, over her lifting the dirty clothes drum off the fire with the barrel of my new .222 rifle with the telescopic sight. But that was miles later.

There's something about fires on roadsides. A kind of remembery permanent feeling you only get when you travel around like us. We never talked about it, but I could tell by the way Fiff unrolled our big rough swag and fussed around finding the best way for our heads to go that she felt the same way as me about camping like this. Our fire at Corinda had the same something about it as our fire at Kynuna.

The trip up to the Gulf was a beaut. Something unusual happened almost very day. The first day there was that row we had and the excitement of setting off on a new adventure. On the second day I stopped to try out the new rifle and 'scope at some kangaroos and we got caught by a bloke on a horse, who galloped up with dogs and told us it was stupid bloody idiots like me who were ruining the country. Fiff got stuck into him about his language in front of ladies and we got away while he was trying to think how to tell us of without swearing. I would have dragged the loud-mouthed coot off his horse and belted hell out of him, only he would probably have belted hell out of me instead. So I took it out on the gearbox of the Landrover for a couple of miles.

The next day we were going along a road too full of holes to go fast and too long and straight to be interesting. Hot and dusty, with trees and nothing else. Not even kangaroos or emus to look out for and point at. Fiff had marked us down to camp that night at Angledool and even filled in her diary to there

17

because of nothing happening. But it was over a week before we got to Angledool, forty miles further on.

We saw a little truck parked at the side of the road with two men leaning on it. We stopped to see if they were all right but they were just getting some beer out of a big ice-box on their truck and invited us to join them. They gave us a can of beer each and told us they were going on a fishing holiday somewhere in Queensland. It was funny to stand on that enormous hot road with no water for miles drinking from an icy can with big wet drops of water on it from the ice-box.

I'd told Fiff there was to be absolutely no talk about crocodiles till we got to where they were. It was ridiculous talking until we'd done it, but when the fishing-holiday blokes asked me I did mention something about us nipping up to the Gulf to pick up a few quidsworth of croc-skins. I suppose a man does get a bit enthusiastic at times.

We had a couple more cans of beer each and yarned around a bit. I got some cans from a carton I'd sneaked into the back of the Landrover the day before and put them in the ice-box to make up for what Fiff and I drank. Then another car came along and had to stop because our 'rover was in the middle of the road. An old bloke and his wife who were going to visit relatives in Bourke. They stayed for a drink and everybody stood around saying how nice beer was on a day like this. Then the old bloke got a bottle of rum out of his car and everybody drank ice-water and rum out of paper cups and said how nice rum was on a day like this too. I had to finish

Fiff's because it was a bit strong for her. She doesn't drink much.

Then a Holden with opal-diggers, three of them, came and joined us. It was amazing how many cars there were on this road, where you could drive all day and not see another vehicle.

All the tins and bottles of beer were put in the ice-box. The bottle of rum was finished off and the old bloke got another one out of his car. His wife said "Now George," and he started to recite some bush poetry, going da-da, da-da, da-da, when he came to the parts a bit ripe for ladies.

Then a drover's truck with things hanging all over it, like an overloaded packhorse, only more, came jangling along. It drove off the road into the trees and stopped. Two men, the cook and the rouseabout, joined us for a drink and then put up a round pen with wire-netting and iron stakes to hold the sheep that were coming.

Cars came and cars went. All of them stopped to see what was going on and had a drink or a few with us. The sheep arrived with dusty men on horses and we all helped lead them into the pen. The drover said they'd only come half the usual distance that day but it didn't matter. They lit a big fire and the drover's cook roasted a whole sheep and chopped bits off with a dirty axe for everybody. Some of us parked our wagons and cars among the trees and Fiff got out our swag to sit on and show everybody we were used to camping like this.

Every time new people arrived they'd ask what the celebration was for, but nobody could tell them. There was a long conference about it but no one could think of a reason for us being there drinking and eating. It was nobody's birthday. It was too far from a Christmas to celebrate that. The drover, who was very easy-going and good at telling jokes, said what about having the celebration just to pass the time, but everybody was short of time and had other things they should have been doing. Then Fiff came up with the answer. She said it was the first time she'd ever seen me stuck for an excuse to drink beer and that was a good enough excuse for her to celebrate. Everybody laughed and the singing and talking started up again. The ladies, there were five of them by this time, sat in a little group by the fire gossiping about their husbands and having drinks brought to them by the drover's cook, who'd been a waiter in a big pub somewhere and knew how to be polite. I talked about crocodiles and opal-digging with the opal-diggers for hours. They were an interesting bunch of listeners.

It must have been well after midnight when Fiff and I crawled into our swag. There were still one or two blokes talking in round-the-fire voices and a groaning old dog came and put himself on the foot of our swag and pushed our feet over to one side. I growled at him to get out of it, Fiff ungrowled at him to stay there and we all went to sleep, with the firelight spreading like sparks in the leaves and branches above us.

2

Best Croc-shooters in Queensland

W E WOKE UP very early in the morning because of all the drover's dogs and there were empty beer cans all over the place. What a mess! It had looked terrific the night before in the firelight among the trees. We had mugs of tea and cold mutton on bread and rolled up our swags. The opal-diggers came over and asked us if we were ready, and I had to tell Fiff I'd promised we'd go to Lightning Ridge with them to opal-dig.

"You can pick up hundreds of quid's worth just lying around on the ground, if you're lucky," I told her. "The opal field hasn't been scratched yet."

She was furious. Not so much about us going opal-digging but because she hadn't been told. She put on her icy-sweet smile and was very polite to the opal-diggers. I was in for it. I even helped her put our pannikins in the box and do up the canopy of the Landrover, but I wasn't getting off that easy. She altered her diary from the day before and didn't even put the tobacco in her side of the cab to roll me smokes on the way.

We said goodbye to the drovers and followed the opal-diggers' Holden out on to the road. After about half an hour Fiff was so curious she had to forgive me so she could ask where Lightning Ridge was, what it was like and would we get any opals and get rich overnight. I couldn't tell her any more about it than I already had, so she un-forgave me and sulked for a bit longer.

We arrived at Lightning Ridge just after twelve o'clock. You can't miss it because it's the only hill sticking up for miles around. If the opal field hadn't been scratched it had certainly been uprooted. Big white mullock-heaps everywhere among the trees and the little winches with buckets on ropes over some of the holes, like old-fashioned wells. There were a couple of shops, a post office, a pub, and a muddy road. We camped two miles out of the town and had to cart water for miles.

Opals are very good-looking things. All the colours you can think of, but mostly red and orange and blue and green. Flashing and deep inside the bits of potch you pick up or dig out round the mullock-heaps. We never got any really valuable proper opals but we got plenty of opalised potch, which looks just as good but isn't pure enough to be called opal. Nearly everyday we heard about someone picking up stones worth hundreds of pounds, but it wasn't us. I kept telling Fiff that it was all baloney and one day took her to see a woman who was supposed to have found an opal worth two thousand pounds lying on the ground, just to prove it was all lies about these fabulous finds.

We found the woman and she'd found a beautiful opal all right. She showed it to us. I can still see it if I close my eyes and remember. It was pearls and diamonds and sunlight and sea all mixed up and compressed into a fragment of electric brilliance. She hadn't picked it up off the ground though. She'd been digging for weeks. We drove back to our camp and scratched and dug till after dark, but found nothing. Up again at first light and into the hillside with a new pick from the store.

The blokes who'd brought us there were half a mile away and we didn't see much of them. They had a puddler. That's a machine with big rubber paddles turning over a sieve. It breaks up the dirt and leaves the rocks and stones to be tested to see if they're opals in disguise or not.

I'd always thought that people getting valuable stones kept them very secret, but not the opal-diggers. Often a car would stop and someone would call out to ask if we'd like to see some opals. They'd gently open little boxes or tins with beautiful opals on cotton-wool in them. They weren't trying to sell the opals, just wanted to show them to people. They're the kind of thing that are meant to be shown round and we never got tired of looking at other people's collections. Just jealous as hell.

In spite of all my work Fiff found the best bit of opal. We had it made into a doublet (that's a thin piece of opal with a potch glued on the bottom; you can't tell them from big opals when they're set in a mounting) and sent it away to be made into an engagement ring for Fiff because she'd never had one. We'd been married over two years but she worked out from Libra and Aquarius in an out-of-date magazine that we were supposed to do that with our most valuable find. I thought I was going to find a better opal anyway, but I never did.

We were opal-diggers for about a week, then in the pub at Lightning Ridge we met a bloke with an old car and a new dog on a string. This bloke had been one of the best professional crocodile-shooters in North Queensland and we started remembering about going croc-shooting again. This bloke told us that they have to drink through long bamboo straws up there in the rivers because of crocodiles. It was no use shooting crocs in the head, he told us, because their brains are in their backbone, same as sharks. You have to shoot them behind the shoulder if you want any results. Sneaking up on them when they're asleep on the mudflats among the mangroves is the best way to get them and my .222 rifle wouldn't even tickle a croc. You had to have a buffalo or elephant gun. He also told us that the crocs tip boats over with one flick of their tails and tear the people in them to bits. Then they bury them in the mud till they're rotten and dig them up and eat them . . . !

He talked for hours about what to do and what not to do, if we valued our lives, but he couldn't tell us the best places to go because it was a few years since he'd given up being a croc-shooter and things were probably a lot different up there now. I remember how much of this we believed, but I think we were believing the stories that fitted in with our plans and ideas and gear at that time, and discarding the unfavourable bits as straight-out dirty lies.

That night we decided that the Lightning Ridge

opal field was worked out and next morning we left for the Gulf of Carpentaria to be croc-shooters again.

We'd been looking forward to crossing the border into Queensland. We crossed it, and that was all there was to it. No officials to ask what we were doing or what we had in the Landrover. Just a sign saying it was the border and a grid across the road. The same road going endlessly over the same flat brown country. And hundreds of miles to go before we reached the croc-country.

We came to a little place called Hebel that reminded Fiff of the Bible. There was a little pub with the most enormous pile of bottles in the world! Thousands of them, piled as high as a roof. It was apparently one of those places where the freight is so high it's not worth returning the empties.

On across plains and through towns and over bridges, and consultations with maps at crossroads.

The closer we got to the croc-country in the north, the more best professional croc-shooters in Queensland we met. At Mitchell we met one who told us that the crocodiles were all shot out; you couldn't get a licence to shoot them, and I wouldn't be allowed to take a woman into the croc-country anyway. So we didn't take any notice of him and only stayed long enough for me to drink a schooner of beer I'd ordered and was having a bit of trouble finishing.

Near Tambo we found a little boy on the road walking. He was carrying a big bag with a baby kangaroo in it and a little bag with all the rest of his things. He'd been going to Brisbane but a truck didn't wait for him and he'd missed the ride he expected. The people who'd brought him out to the main road had gone back and he didn't know what to do. His father was 'roo-shooting for meat on a cattle-run, fifty miles up a side road. Fiff told him he was a brave little man and I asked him what he was going to be when he grew up and he said, "A man." He probably will be, too.

It was a hell of a road in to his father's camp, even for the Landrover. It took hours, creeping through wash-outs and over rotten bridges. The boy's father and his mate were getting ready to go out shooting when we drove up. He growled at the boy for coming back, thanked us for bringing him, and invited us to go out with them that night. It was a good opportunity to try out the new .222 and 'scope and keep my eye in, so I accepted.

So we went spotlighting kangaroos. Fiff sat in the front with the driver in case she got in the road and I stood on the back with the rifle, the boy's father and the spotlight. We saw about eighty 'roos — and got twenty-seven. Every time the father fired at a 'roo he missed and I shot it with the .222. I'm nothing spectacular as a rifle-shot but this bloke was something terrible. And he said he hit every one of them and they'd have dropped within a few yards anyway. His rifle was too light and his spotlight had no range. I didn't like to tell him that I'd shot 'roos professionally for two years because I was only a guest. I was glad to get away from there next morning because he was making such a botch of cleaning up the dead 'roos that I could hardly control myself.

That day we met another best professional croc-shooter, who told us that the rivers in the Western

Gulf were swarming with crocodiles and the best way to get them was in big traps made of wire mesh. He'd got a twenty-seven foot crocodile, full of human bones, in a mysterious lagoon where no birds live and no animals drink and no people go. He wouldn't say where it was.

Next day, two hundred miles further on, we met another best croc-shooter in a pub. He was telling us about crocodiles snatching the heads off horses and bulls when another best croc-shooter came along the bar to join in. Once they got started they forgot all about us; comparing places they'd been and numbers of crocs they'd shot. Best professional croc-shooter number one would say, "Of course that doesn't include the time me and Andy Meikin shot four hundred and eighty freshies and nine fourteen-foot salties in the Normanby one trip."

And best professional croc-shooter number two would drink from his glass and say, "Yeah, that's okay when you're after the little stuff, but I only go for the big ones. A dozen salties, anything up to twenty-foot, was a good night when I shot the Roper a few years back, and that was working on my own, mind you."

And best professional croc-shooter number one would say, "Not bad goin'. Don't bother much with the big stuff myself, but I pulled a twenty-two footer out of a waterhole thirty yards long and ten feet deep near the head of the Leichhardt the year before last. Good skin too, first grade."

Best professional croc-shooter number two replied: "Can't have been much water left in the waterhole when you dragged that one out on the bank to skin it." Fiff and I looked at each other with our it's-time-to-get-going look and got going. Weren't there any small crocodiles for us to practise on?

The road got longer the further we went along it. Flat and bare. The whole world was made out of dust, with two wheel-tracks to show where cars had been. We'd got off the main road somehow and our road maps didn't know where we were. We camped and drove all next day. The only things that changed were the numbers on the speedo and we passed endless hours guessing when they were going to flick over to another number. We got quite good at it.

We found Julia Creek just before dark one night. Everything was drenched in dust and our poor old Landrover looked very tired and ruffled and thirsty.

The road from Julia Creek to Cloncurry was so bad that we went across country along the railway line. I thought we were never going to get across some of the gullies and rough places, but the bits in between were smooth and hard and we made fair time.

Mount Isa for the night and next day out in to the Gulf Country on a quaint little road that goes up and down and round the sides of hills. Not really very hilly, but just nicely rumpled after the flat dead country we'd been driving over for the last few days. And millions of enormous red anthills sticking up everywhere, like spikes to frighten flying saucers away, Fiff said.

Everywhere we camped the crows woke us up in the morning. They're very wise birds, crows. I was almost certain one of them was following me all the way from New South Wales, just to make sure I never slept in. They know when you're thinking of getting the rifle out. But it's no good just pretending to think of it, they can tell that too.

There were lots of birds and plants we didn't know the names or habits of, so Fiff wrote "Books of Queensland Plants and Flowers and Animals and Birds and Lizards" in the THINGS TO BE SENT FOR part of the diary.

At a little pub with a cool and creaky verandah we were told that there were crocodiles in a creek fifty miles further on. We might get one if we went very quietly along the bank. So back into the waggon and drive madly on to where the road crossed a creek on a bridge of big old logs. It was very disappointing. We'd come thousands of miles across a country too big to even think of all at once, to a stupid trickle of water with a few trees growing along it. And swarms of big hard scratchy nervous brown grasshoppers flying everywhere and not looking where they were going. The creek didn't look very sinister or crocodily after all the stories we'd been hearing, but we weren't taking any chances.

Whenever Fiff wants to embarrass me she reminds me about creeping warily down the bank of that creek to fill the tea billy, with the rifle loaded and cocked, ready for attacking crocodiles. Later that day I sneaked along the creek bank with all the stealth of an earthquake. I saw nothing.

The next day we arrived at Yaloginda. We were at last in the heart of the croc-country in the Gulf of Carpentaria. It sounds a lot more impressive than it

31

looked. Buildings, about half a dozen of them, tossed out on the brown plain like thrown dice. The store was two hundred yards away from the pub, and the post office, garage and police station at ragged intervals in between. The first settlers must have thought Yaloginda was going to go ahead and all spaces would be filled up with shops. They were filled up with rubbish and saltbush. The town seemed to have been there before the river — the Manara River, deep and swirly, slooging brownly past with islands of thick green mangrove splitting the lazy current. Our map showed Yaloginda to be right on the coast but there was no sight of the sea. The mouth of the river was four miles across the plain and the country was so flat that we seldom saw the sea in all the time we spent in the Gulf.

Darcy Something-or-other (a great big impossible foreign name) was the best professional croc-shooter in Queensland, they told us at the pub. He was based in Yaloginda but not due in from a river for a couple of days. This Darcy's mate had gone off somewhere to be a lighthousekeeper and Darcy was on his own. He'd probably be only too happy to take us with him croc-shooting. After all the best professional croc-shooters in Queensland we'd already met, I wasn't going to commit myself till I'd seen him.

We drove to Burketown, seventy miles away, for a look to pass the time and perhaps meet an even better best professional croc-shooter in Queensland who would be only too happy to take us with him croc-shooting. It was obvious that we would have to be shown the ropes by someone who knew them.

There was nothing at Burketown. We camped the night and went back the next day to Yaloginda.

Darcy was there.

3

An Ordinary Looking Bloke

SOMEONE POINTED HIM OUT TO ME in the pub. He looked even less like my idea of a professional croc-shooter than the others had, except that he was barefooted. There was no big knife hanging on his belt. No rifle leaning on the bar beside him. No big scars or missing arms or legs. Just an ordinary-looking bloke with hair a little longer than most people's.

I hate asking people for things, especially strangers, but the missus threatened to ask him herself. So I went up to him and asked if me and the wife could go on a croc-shooting trip with him. He was quite happy to take us, but we couldn't tell that at first. He was a Czechoslovakian or Yugoslavian or something and it was hard to tell what he was saying or thinking. He'd been croc-shooting here for ten years and talked as though he'd learned English from a book, but hadn't been able to practise his conversation much because of being in the bush all the time. He pulled faces to help him get the words out and it was quite flattering to have someone go to such a lot of trouble to tell you something. I think he still thought in his native language because you'd often see him just going to say something and then there'd be a pause for concentration while he worked it out in English before saying it. He'd been mostly in the company of men and had a pretty thorough grounding in bad language but he was too polite to make use of it. When there was a woman around he hardly ever spoke. It gave us the impression that he was surly and unfriendly at first, but he was only kind of washing out his vocabulary and hanging it up to dry. After a day or so he talked quite freely and we had many long interesting discussions with him.

I remember Darcy's un-outback appearance, and how I learned later that my imagined croc-shooter was as spurious as the water-bag hanging on the front of our Landrover. Darcy was real outback and carried his water in a 44-gallon drum. I wanted to take the water-bag off the Landrover when I discovered how paltry it was, but Fiff wouldn't hear of it and it stayed there as a reminder of the time when we planned to travel the Gulf from one end to the other with one water-bag of water.

Darcy had the big "blitz" army truck, loaded with sacks and drums and boxes. Except for a frail-looking plywood dinghy the whole load looked as though it was ready to be taken to a rubbish dump and tipped off.

He also had a big young dog called Pruszkowic that you couldn't tell the breed of. Darcy wrote the name out for me so I know it's right, but it sounds more

like "Prooshkovits". The dog rode in the cab beside
Darcy and felt the same way about the blitz as Fiff
did about our Landrover. Pruszkowic waited outside
the pub for Darcy and looked after the blitz. All the
other dogs wandered in and out of the bar but Darcy
told us his dog didn't drink because one of them had
to stay sober to see that they got back to camp all
right. I asked Darcy what Pruszkowic meant but he
wouldn't say in front of Fiff and I always forgot to
ask him when she wasn't there. It must have been
something pretty shocking because Darcy came out
with some real rippers at times and didn't seem to
mind Fiff hearing, though he never indulged in ordinary swearing when she was around. More than I can
say for myself.

The day we first met Darcy he was going to the
Nicholson River and said for us to follow him. It was
about eighty miles. He had one or two things to do
first, like leaving the bar and getting into his truck
and driving off. He already had his drums of petrol
and bags of salt and supplies loaded, but he doddered
around till I was just about frantic. His casual atti-
tude to croc-shooting and his reluctance to get started
were comforting in a way and I was already beginning to have a bit of confidence in him. He was
certainly not a show-off. But after all the looking-
forward-to we'd done, all the miles we'd travelled and
all the stories we'd heard, it was hard not to be
impatient. When he finally cranked his blitz and
drove off along the dirt road I couldn't help crowding. We followed in a great deluge of dust right under
the tailboard of the rattling blitz.

Two hours on the road and half an hour across the

plain and we arrived at the Nicholson. We parked the vehicles on the bank of the green-deep river among Mitchell grass and trailing paperbarks. It was a real crocodily place, with dark mysterious corners under the banks and leaning trees. I began to feel like a real croc-shooter.

We began to unload the gear. Now that we were actually there I was no longer impatient. We were at last going to shoot crocodiles — or at least see them shot.

But Darcy's gear! Even Fiff noticed. I'd had misgivings about the little boat that we easily lifted off the back of the blitz and slid down the bank to shallow water (to let the cracks soak tight so it wouldn't leak so much) but that was nothing. He got out two rusty rifles, a .303 and a .22, that you could hardly work the clogged bolts of. He leaned them against a tree and one of them fell in the dirt, and stayed there till I picked it up and sneaked a look at it. I'd seen a few rifles in my time but I'd never known one fired in such a neglected condition as that .303. He got out a knife and stuck it in the ground beside the rifles. It was sharp enough but alarmingly small for such enormous, ferocious things as the crocodiles we'd heard about. Then a spotlight about the size of a torch-head that fitted on his forehead with an elastic strap and ran off the blitz-battery. It was pale and flickery just to look at and it was hard not to offer to fix it for him. There was nothing really wrong with it, just neglect.

Then Darcy went into the trees and changed into his working-clothes — a kind of baggy napkin he tied round his waist with a piece of shreddy rope. It looked like a length of faded, gaily-coloured chair-cover. (Fiff identified it in whispers as a piece of curtain material.) You could tell he was used to wearing it because of the way it fitted his sunburn. He wasn't a big man, or a small one. He stood about five-foot-ten and had wiry, jumpy muscles in his back and arms. He had long blond hair and was somewhere between thirty and forty years old. It was hard to tell. But there was no mistake about him being fit and hard. There was a kind of economy about him that was a lot less inspiring in his gear than it was in Darcy.

Fiff lit the fire in the best place and began making a damper to go with the billy of tea that was coming up. Darcy threw a heap of rope off his truck and began to untangle it. I saw there was a rusty iron shaft, about eight inches of three-quarter mild steel with a big flat barbed point at one end. The rope Darcy was shaking loops and knots out of was spliced to a ring at the middle of this thing.

Darcy looked up at me watching. "If you are going to be croc-shooter you should be understanding this. It is my harpoon."

I tried to look as interested as I was and he went over to the blitz and got a long straight pole out from under all the stuff that cluttered the tray. It was about fifteen feet long and had a shark-hook bound to the thin end.

"This hook is to bring a dead croc off the bottom in shallow water," he explained. "When you kill a croc he sinks quickly to the bottom. That is why you must be coming very close to him before you shoot and very quick to snatch his leg or snout afterwards."

"What if they're not properly dead?" I asked.

"In all things you must use your sense," he replied. "But when you have a big bloke in deep water you will lose him if you shoot him, because you cannot get him to your boat, or even hold him up from sinking. So you must use your harpoon. There are many kinds of harpoon, but this one is good enough for me."

He picked up the iron quill and tried to fit the smooth end of the shaft into a hole in the thick end of the pole, but it was clogged with mud where he'd been poling his dinghy away from banks or something. He began to dig it clear with a piece of stick.

"This fits into the hole and is sliding out when you stick the croc in the neck. That is the best place to strike him. Then you will have him on the end of your rope and you have only to wait your chance to shoot him."

He fitted the quill into the end of the pole and demonstrated how it worked by stabbing the quill lightly into a log. It was a very simple and effective-looking device. Exciting.

"That is the theory and it works most of the time. There are many interesting variations and you must be prepared for it to go wrong," he said.

"Doesn't the croc attack the boat when you stick that thing into him?"

"Not usually, or I would not be here. But a croc could be easily breaking your boat by accident when he flicks his tail or head trying to get away. His main thought is to escape into deep water when he is attacked."

"Have you ever had a croc smash your boat or attack you?" I asked.

"No, only once I had an accident with my harpoon. The quill would not come free from the pole and the croc swung the pole round and was knocking me from the boat."

It looked as though Darcy was going to leave the story at that so I said, "What happened?"

"I went into the water and got quickly back into my boat," he said.

"Did you get the croc?"

"Yes, but I lost my light and had to come 300 miles to get another one."

"Don't you carry a spare light?" I couldn't help asking.

"If I had looked after my harpoon correctly I would not have needed a spare light," he said.

Hell!

While we were having pannikins of tea and chunks of fresh damper Fiff asked Darcy if he often taught people how to be croc-shooters.

'Many people come with me because they are so curious about crocodiles. Not many of them come two times and most of them I do not like."

"What do you do, kick them out?" asked Fiff embarrassingly.

"No," said Darcy. "There is no need for me to be sending them away. There are places where I can take them that only a good man or a crocodile can live in."

"Will you take us to a place like that when you're tired of us?" asked Fiff earnestly.

"No," said Darcy. "Your husband is not a sightseer.

He wants to be a crocodile-shooter so I will teach him. When he is ready he will not be happy to remain with me. He will go away to rivers to try out his new knowledge."

"How long will it take, Darcy?"

"You could shoot crocodiles for many years and still know nothing about them. One man can learn more in one instant than another learns in a lifetime."

"But when will we be proper croc-shooters?" insisted Fiff.

"As soon as you shoot a crocodile," replied Darcy. And that was all he'd say about it.

He was a hard man to understand. But the more we saw of him and spoke to him, the more convinced I was that he was a man who knew what he was doing. Only that gear of his had me puzzled. It was many weeks before I began to understand.

It was reassuring to learn that Darcy was mainly interested in the smaller freshwater crocodiles at the moment. Johnstone River crocodiles, they're called. Grow to about ten feet and aren't dangerous to swimming humans. They eat fish mostly, but will have a go at anything that's lying around and can be grabbed. They'd give you a very nasty bite if you mishandled one. I was quite happy to start on the little ones. There was the odd big "salty" in the Nicholson but Darcy wasn't expecting to get on to them.

"We will make a lot of noise getting the freshies," he explained.

Darcy and I hung mosquito nets for later and as the evening was drawing close we prepared the dinghy for shooting that night — or rather Darcy did. I just watched and passed him things.

He bailed the water out of the dinghy and jammed the milk-tin bailer under the middle seat. Then he folded sacks on the seats and laid the rifles, loaded and ready, on them.

"So that there's no knocking on the wood of the boat when I pick up a rifle to shoot."

Then he coiled the harpoon rope neatly in the bow and stuck the quill ready in the crack between the front seat and the side of the dinghy. The knife he put in the opposite crack. A big hatchet on a sack in the bottom of the boat. Then I passed him the battery out of the blitz, which he put under the front seat ready to clip the spotlight on to. The harpoon pole laid along the boat and sticking out over the back. "Croc-box" under the back seat with spare ammunition, light bulbs, torch, mosquito repellent, matches and odds and ends. And the big hand-made paddle Darcy used instead of oars or outboard motor. A plastic jar of water from the big drum on Darcy's truck. The river here was tidal and salty, though there was no sign of any current. The little dinghy looked small and overloaded already.

It was nearly dark. A feed of something or other, a pannikin of tea. Darcy lights his carbide light so we can find the place when we come back. Pruszkowic is told to look after the camp, and goes to sit importantly by the blitz.

"Of course your wife can come. Why not?"

The first stars and mosquitoes. Better wear long sleeves and pants. It might get cold later. The birds are quiet. A splash out in the river. Frogs croak.

Got the tobacco? It's time!

Fiff and me on the back seat, Darcy in the bow. He

pushes us away from the bank with the paddle and fixes the light over his lumpy old hat. Out on the still river the dinghy turns slowly on black solid water. Hell, it's small! Why doesn't he have a bigger boat?

The light spears out across the river and rakes the banks on either side, up and down. (Which is upstream, anyway?) Then he picks up the paddle and begins to pull us along with big easy strokes. Not a ripple or a swirl, two strokes on one side, two on the other. It's like sliding through space. The thin brilliance of the spotlight poking its finger in to the black corners of the overhanding river. And the speed, only evident from the sliding of the flanking trees across the stars. Too fast to be going into something that should be tackled with caution and preparation.

It was like being forced into a decision. I would have liked just to sit in the dinghy for a while to get used to the atmosphere.

Hundreds of fish, swirling suddenly in the light away from the dinghy, sloshing loudly out in the dark. Noises around us. The wump! wump! wump! of a wallaby frightened enough to run and curious enough to stay, compromising by bounding along the bank. Yippings, churkings, raspings, and crackings.

The light flicks back to a place it's just swept past, and there are the unmistakable eyes of a crocodile. Brilliantly red in all that vast lack of colour. No horny head or curved tail, not even the eyes themselves. Just a blaze of red smouldering in the reeds at the far bank.

The dinghy glides over the distance towards the unblinking stare at the end of the light, Darcy leaning forward in the bow of our headlong dinghy without a falter in the dip and switch of the big paddle.

Closer, right up to the thing. Darcy steers expertly with the paddle in one hand and picks up the .22 with the other. Still the eyes are all you can see. Darcy lays the paddle across his knees and raises the rifle. His shoulder blots out the sight of the croc's eyes. We must be nearly on top of it! All of a sudden the anticipation of this moment becomes a bellyful of reluctance. I lean back in the seat and clutch at the side of the dinghy.

Then the shot, a glimpse of a white belly floating in the light. Darcy hooks under it with the edge of the paddle as it begins to sink and grabs it by the snout. He pulls its head over the side of the boat and reaches to grope for the hatchet. Two chops behind the head severs its spine. He passes his grip round the jaws back along the gunwale to me. My hand takes a twitching nervous grip on the cold snout. I lift it in two heaves over the side of the dinghy and lay it out in the bottom of the boat.

A six-foot freshy. I kept reaching down in the dark to feel the cold scales of my first crocodile while Darcy rolled a smoke and spoke quietly to us about where we might pick up another one or two.

Fiff told me she wasn't scared because of me being there, just a little nervous about the suddenness of the noises because of it being so dark. Hell!

A mile or so further up the river we got two more freshies and heard what Darcy said was "a big bloke" crash down a bank ahead into the water with a splash as though the world had fallen in. Then we came to a place where the river had dried up. We had to get out and drag the boat through a hundred yards of mud and shallow water to where the river was deep again. Darcy said that most of these rivers dried up into a series of long lagoons in the dry season.

We got six freshies altogether that night, all in pretty much the same style as the first one. It was nearly three o'clock in the morning when we arrived back at the place where Darcy's carbide light was flickering weakly on the bank to mark our camp. Pruszkowic came over to report that all was well and have a look at our crocs. We had mugs of tea and slices of Yaloginda bread, then crawled into our swags under the mosquito nets. Fiff snuggled happily around inside my arm till we were warm and comfortable. Then she whispered one of our special sayings and went to sleep. I lay there for a while thinking about croc-shooting.

I'd been hunting things like pigs and deer and kangaroos ever since I was old enough to pinch my old man's rifle when he was away, but this was like no hunting I'd ever imagined. Wait till we got stuck into some of those "big blokes" of Darcy's!

What a strange bloke he was. A real croc-shooter!

In the morning Darcy showed Fiff and me how to open up the crocs, skin them, and scrape and salt the skins. He told us that hornbacks are different from belly-skins and not worth quite so much. That the salting and storing are very important.

I wanted to pitch in and have a go at it but he said I'd get plenty of practice later and the best thing to do for the time being was just watch. It took him about two and a half hours to skin and scrape and salt the six crocs we'd got the night before, explaining everything as he went.

After lunch we loaded everything on and into the vehicles, crossed the Nicholson at the dried up ford a mile downstream, and drove for a couple of hours across country to a sandy river, where Darcy said we should get quite a lot of freshies. We camped on a sloping bank at the end of a line of rocks across a dry part of the river. Darcy and I went out that night and got thirteen.

Two of them were stuffers, only a year or two old. A stuffer is anything from nine inches to a couple of feet long. You drift the dinghy right up to them, grab them hard and quick round the neck and put them in the sack in the bottom of the boat, careful to tie the top of the sack because even at that age they can give you a nasty bite. Darcy skinned them in a special way and cured the hide and head with salt and mounted them. He made a very professional looking job of them, too. Sold them for three bob an inch to people round the Gulf or travellers. I was surprised that he wasn't using arsenic or something to cure his stuffer-skins, but he said the first ones he ever did, seven years before, were as good as the day he finished them. He later taught Fiff how to do them and she became as good at it as Darcy himself.

I was going to have a go at the skinning this time and I was up at dawn, knife like a razor, ready to get started. I learned something that day. The disgrace of cutting a hole in my first skin. And the next. Nervous of Darcy's disapproval. Bellies and hornbacks.

"Any crocodile less than sixteen inches across the belly is a hornback."

Open it up down the belly to the tip of the tail and square under the legs like Darcy showed us. Open the belly-skins above the second row of buttons, high on each side down to the top of the tail and down the tops of the legs. Keep them square. Knife it off carefully all the way. Watch it round the legs and under the jaw. Every knife cut can cost you a quid.

"You should use your knife a little blunt until you learn the feeling of it," said Darcy kindly. "You can scrape off meat but you cannot mend cuts in the hide."

Darcy used two knives. A little straight one for opening-up and a big curved one for knifing-off, of which he used only the tip, holding it like a fountain pen.

The dinghy upside-down in the shade ("Never let the sunlight shine on your skins or they will get scaleslip") with Fiff up to her knees at the edge of the river, scraping the meat off the skins with a thing like a big sharp fish-scaler. The flesh is white, like tough fish. Darcy's eaten it and says any meat is the best you can get if you can't get anything else. Pruszkowic won't look at it, even cooked. Don't blame him.

Give Fiff a spell with the scraping. There's only three left to skin. She's just mucking around down there. Only done two. Hell, but it's tough going! Harder work than the skinning. Poor old Fiff must have had it. Look at her sitting on the bank trying not to show it.

"Make us a billy of tea, Mum."

Scraping, scraping. Try and keep it vigorous, it comes off easier that way — like scrubbing. Drift back into pulling at the meat as though the scraper's a hairbrush, till you notice you're not getting anywhere and rip into it again as long as you can keep it up.

Get the file out of the Landrover and sharpen the scraper, you fool. It's blunt. Take your time while your arm has a rest from the scraping. Notice how the edge has been filed at an angle on one side and left flat on the other? Follow that. Till your arm gets tired from filing and back to scraping.

A bit easier, but you've cut a nick in the skin with the scraper. It's too sharp now. Take a bit of the edge off on this rock. Get on with the scraping. Try using your left hand — no good.

Got one finished! Wash the bits of meat off it and throw it into the shallow water near the ones that haven't been done yet. Next one. Sweat and hair in a man's eyes. Darcy's nearly finished skinning the last one.

A pannikin of tea and a smoke.

"I'll scrape the rest while you do the salting, if you like, Darcy." (What the hell are you saying!)

But Darcy takes a turn at the scraping and makes it look easy. You do the next one. There *must* be an easier way of doing it. Wire brush? A blade in a thing like a safety-razor so you won't cut the skin? Scraping the skin over a blade bolted on to the blitz? Try cooking it of? Ants? No; just keep on scraping.

They're all done. Arm on fire and a back like a shearer. Now the salting. Spread them out on the grass in the shade, biggest on the bottom. Dig handfuls of fine salt out of the bag with cuts stinging and spread it on. Put plenty on, salt's cheap compared to croc-skins at six and six an inch across the widest part. Make sure to rub it well into all the folds and edges. Scatter a couple of double handfuls over it for good measure and lay the next biggest skin on the top. Same again.

Fold the belly-flaps and legs in and roll them up from the head in the way Darcy does. Keep that salt in. Get Fiff to hold the sack and pack them in. Throw a couple of handfuls of spilt salt on each layer. Put the sack on the blitz and cover it with more sacks for extra shade. Hell, they're heavy. Darcy has been watching and nods approvingly.

"You will not be difficult to teach," he said, "because you are anxious to learn."

What's the time? One o'clock. Flop on the swag beside Fiff and roll a smoke. Darcy might decide not to go out tonight. A flaming joker's got to rest some time. None of those expert croc-shooters we met on the way up here said anything about scraping the skins. Shooting them's the easy part.

Have a feed and a couple of hours' rest under the mosquito net away from the flies. Read up on Fiff's diary and correct the spelling then start prowling around the camp, making sure everything's ready to be got ready for shooting that night.

4

Pruszkowic

WE STAYED FOUR DAYS at the sandy river, and got forty-one croc-skins there. Then we headed off across the shimmering plain and cast out among scattered bush till we found a little lagoon Darcy knew about. Fifty yards long and twenty across in a green circle of trees. Darcy said we should get fifteen or twenty freshies there before we went back to Yaloginda to send the skins away. The water looked muddy enough to walk on, but what we'd been drinking was brackish and rusty. We saw about half a dozen crocs surface while we were looking for a place to camp. I was surprised how easy it was going to be to get them in such a small body of water. I had another surprise coming. We lit a fire at the edge of the water at the shallow end of the waterhole and slung the mosquito nets under a big forked paperback that Fiff discovered was good to sit in.

Darcy got his old radio hooked up to the Landrover

battery and Fiff made friends with a little waving-hand lizard that came to listen.

Darcy got a four-inch gill-net out of the confusion on the blitz and we strung it across the centre of the lagoon.

"Once a crocodile touches a net his teeth are caught and he rolls up in it and drowns himself."

Pruszkowic found a big yellow goanna under a log and grabbed it by the tail. He got a badly bitten nose out of the encounter and Darcy got the goanna ready for stuffing.

That night we shone the spotlight round the lagoon and lit up eyes like the lights of a city. I reckoned there must have been about fifty crocs there, but Darcy said twenty-five. It was a great sight all the same. We paddled around that lagoon for two hours but the crocs wouldn't let us get near them. There was a deep rumbling in the water that Darcy said was the crocs roaring underwater. We shot five, but they all sank before we could reach them. The lagoon was far too deep for us to reach the bottom with a pole. It was very flattening. We went back to the camp to make plans.

The best way to get those crocs, Darcy said, was to shoot them and wait till they floated to the surface.

"It takes a few days, depending on the deepness and on the temperature of the water. If we get to them quickly when they rise to the surface we can save the skins. But we must be careful not to leave dead crocs floating in the waterhole because it could make us unfavourable with the station manager, who might be refusing his permission for us to shoot crocodiles across his country."

Next morning we pulled in the net. There were only two small crocs in it, and two beautiful big barramundi. Good eating, too. Even Darcy was surprised to find these aristocratic fish in such a muddy little lagoon. One of the crocs had wrapped the net around a stake and we had to tear it free to get out. So Darcy told me to go down the lagoon and see how many crocs I could shoot while he mended the net.

"Count please how many you kill so we can expect that many to arise later to be skinned," he said.

I must have looked a bit silly, dashing around with delight. I'd been bursting to try out my .222 rifle and 'scope on the crocs. This was just the opportunity. I found a good ambush on the bank and by that night I'd shot thirteen crocs I was sure of and three I wasn't. They weren't lying on the surface any more. It doesn't take them long to wake up. They'd come up, two little green ridges of eyes and snout, just long enough to get a breath. Then they'd go down again without a ripple. You'd have to be quick to get a shot in and they come up in the most unexpected places. If they surfaced in one place without being shot at they'd try it a second time, otherwise they shifted around all over the place.

I never actually saw one surface. They're so subtle about it they just appear and vanish again like impressions. Fifteen minutes seemed to be roughly the time they stayed under, but Darcy said it varies with the size and age of the crocs, from a few minutes for little freshies to an hour or more for a big old salty. It's less, though, if they're wounded or very excited. It was a good opportunity to study the crocs at close hand and I learned a lot about them that day.

This method of shooting may look a bit callous. Well, I've shot thousands of 'roos and deer and pigs and I still always get annoyed at wounding one and do my best to track it down and finish it off. But I've never heard of anyone feeling like that about a crocodile. There's something about them. You can't feel sorry for them — there's something evil about them.

The next day Darcy told me that if you shoot any croc in the end of the nose and hit the valve there it can't stay under the water or it drowns. It has to come out on the bank, the same as crocs that are sick or badly wounded. So I was to try and nose-shoot the ones I'd missed the day before. We didn't want to have to wait around too long for crocs to float to the surface.

I sat up in a tree this day because it was a better angle to shoot from and the crocs couldn't see where I was. Any movement on the bank is silhouetted against a background of sky in that flat country and a croc has incredible eyesight. My targets were no bigger than a sixpence perched on the end of a croc's nose. I missed a lot of shots. But when I did hit one it was quite spectacular — the croc would disappear in the splash, the same as a miss, but after a few seconds he'd come periscoping to the surface and thrash round and round the lagoon and then climb out on to the bank. I'd yell out to Darcy who'd come paddling down in the dinghy and finish it of with his .22, which didn't go off sometimes.

Occasionally I'd only nick the croc's nose and he'd drive and bury his head in the mud on the bottom of the lagoon. Then, just when I'd give him up, he'd come thrashing up. Then he'd dive again just as

Darcy got there with the harpoon. Then, just as Darcy was leaving, he'd come bursting up again and they'd chase each other round and round till Darcy got a quill into the croc. And don't they snap at that rope! I'd hate to have even a freshy attack me in the water. A man wouldn't stand a chance. Darcy has a theory that the only reason freshwater crocodiles aren't dangerous to humans could be that they don't grow big enough.

"A salty up to ten feet long isn't dangerous to humans or cattle either — usually."

It was days before the dead crocs started floating up, but fun waiting.

"Let's have a discussion," Fiff would say when there wasn't much doing.

"What will we discuss about?" Darcy would ask.

"Tell us about rivers," Fiff would say.

And Darcy would tell us about the Roper or the Limmen, or some other river he'd croc'd in.

He'd spent two years at some foreign university before the war loused things up for him. He was carted away to be a soldier when he was seventeen. I don't know whose side he was on, but he had a job leading patrols and taking prisoners as far as I could make out from what he'd say about it. Apparently he was wounded and captured a couple of times. Then he deserted and was court-martialled and let off instead of getting a medal for something brave he'd done.

In the ten years he'd been in the Gulf he'd learned more about Australia than we knew, in a lot of ways. Makes a man think. Anyway we always ran out of time before we ran out of things to say, and we always ended up on croc-shooting. We never found out what actually started Darcy on croc-shooting, but he'd been on his own most of the time. He'd had mates from time to time but apparently they'd been unable to stand the solitude as well as Darcy and had gone off to take jobs closer to civilisation and other people. One bloke had left him up on the Cape York Peninsula and taken four hundred croc-skins into town to sell. That was the last Darcy ever heard of him.

During one of these discussions Darcy told us how some of the Myall aborigines in Arnhem Land cross the rivers. When families of abos on walkabout have to cross a river, they stop half a mile before they get to it and have a breather and sort themselves out. Then they run to the river, dive straight in and swim across. The oldest and weakest get left behind and are the only ones left in the water by the time any crocs around get into action.

"A croc will nearly always take the last horse or cow or person in a bunch."

It's a handy way to weed out the weak, but I wouldn't like to be an old abo — or, come to think of it, it wouldn't be so bad at that. At least they don't kick you out of the family as a reward for growing old, and leave you to die among strangers, like we do. An abo knows what to expect and why to expect it. There's nothing personal about it.

Darcy told us, too, about an eighteen-foot croc parading up and down in the river in front of a blacks' camp with a screaming girl held in its jaws, ducking her under every now and again and then holding her up kicking and screaming again. When the croc got tired of this it closed its jaws and sank. The last they saw of the girl she was sinking slowly into the spreading stain of her own blood.

That story kept me quiet for a bit then I asked Darcy, "Why didn't you shoot the croc?"

"I could not have hit the croc without the danger of hitting the girl," he replied. "And my eyes were almost blinded by what they were seeing."

That had happened nearly six years before when Darcy had been trapped by the wet season for three months and was initiated into a tribe of natives on an Arnhem Land river.

Pruszkowic always joined us when we were talking, and listened politely with his eyes to whoever was speaking. He never got in the way though, because he was a dog, and dogs who interrupt the boss when he's talking get sent to sit under the blitz, like a small boy being sent to bed.

Fiff and I were just beginning to realise how good a dog Pruszkowic was. We didn't notice at first because of him being so polite. And Darcy never bragged about him — or anything. No snake could come near our camp without Pruszkowic warning us. I think he actually used to patrol them. He became especially protective about Fiff and whenever she left the camp or went for a swim, Pruszkowic would go importantly first and watch all the time for dangers, real or suspected. Darcy didn't mind his dog spending so much time with Fiff. He encouraged it.

I'll always remember him saying, "The greatest pleasure for my dog is looking after his people, and the greater the responsibility the greater is his pleasure. He is better at looking after your wife than we are, because you see he is never thinking of other things. For Pruszkowic a world full of dangers is the best kind of world. When he has no one to protect a dog is only half a dog."

I took Pruszkowic hunting pigs one afternoon and we caught a monstrous old sow, which I hung in a tree so we could pick up the meat the next day if we wanted. Then I got lost on the flat plain and couldn't find my way back to the lagoon. Pruszkowic and I had a bit of an argument about which direction it was in and I won. We found the wheel-marks of the Landrover and blitz in the long grass and followed them in the moonlight for a couple of miles, till I saw by the tyre treads of the 'rover on a claypan that we were going in the wrong direction. Pruszkowic, who'd been walking behind, took over and marched in front as soon as I started going the right way.

When we got back to camp I told Darcy and Fiff we'd got on to a pig that took us a long time to catch and kill. It wasn't worth mentioning anything to them about being lost, especially Fiff. She has a stubborn belief that I can do anything.

The next day we went in the Landrover to get the pig I'd hung in the tree and it took us a hell of a time to find it. All that country looks the same. We salted about forty pounds of pork but never got to try any of it. It was flogged off the back of Darcy's blitz by some ringers when we and they were coincidentally in Yaloginda a week later.

On another little walkabout I was going for a stroll in the moonlight when Pruszkowic started barking his come-and-have-a-look-at-this bark in the distance. I had no rifle with me, nor even a knife, but it was a fair way back to the camp. I ran towards the barking, picking up a good hefty lump of wood on the way. It might only be a goanna in a tree.

Pruszkowic was running round and round a six-foot croc in the mud at the dried-up end of a shallow waterhole. I won't go into the details but I managed to kill the croc with my lump of wood in the finish. I strolled back into camp with it over my shoulder and casually dumped it by the water to be skinned next morning. Fiff and Darcy were both waiting for me to tell them how I'd caught a big freshy with my bare hands but I nonchalantly talked about other things as though nothing had happened. I felt a bit lousy about cheating Pruszkowic out of his rightful share of credit in the affair, so I confessed some of the details to Fiff. She called me an old lizard-skinner and we had a happy afternoon planning what might be going to happen.

I later overheard Darcy telling them in the Yaloginda pub about me catching a six-footer with obvious pride. Darcy doesn't know how to whisper.

The dead crocs started coming to the surface of the lagoon in twos and threes and we were kept fairly busy skinning and scraping for a day or two. When we reckoned we'd got most of them Darcy decided we should take our skins to Yaloginda. It was getting too moonlight for spotlighting crocs effectively anyway. So we headed across country in a direction that only Darcy knew.

Just before the dirt road that led to the Nicholson

River crossing, Darcy's blitz dropped its front wheels into a hollow in the grass and plunged its nose into a bank as though it was trying to blow it. There was no damage done but his motor had stalled. Darcy never used the self-starter because he was always saving the battery for spotlighting and his starter-motor had seized up. I tried to pull him out backwards with the Landrover but couldn't budge him. It became a decision whether it would be less trouble to take the starter off and free it, or dig a space in the bank so we could use the crank handle. We decided to do both in case one didn't work. I dug and Darcy undid the starter, unclogged it and put it back on again. We both finished at the same time and used the crank handle because Darcy hated wasting battery-power. He backed out of the hole with a great roaring and jouncing and skidding, and we carried on.

When we arrived at the Nicholson crossing the tide was in and the water had backed up chest-deep. There was nothing to do but wait for it to go out again. We backed the vehicles into the shade of trees and had a brew of tea and cold barramundi on Fiff's camp-oven bread.

Fiff was still sad about our Landrover not being able to pull Darcy's blitz out of that hole. So I cheered her up a bit by making a slight adjustment to what I said was a slipped timing-cog in the transmission-case and told her it was a wonder the 'rover went at all with that not working properly.

Putting the Landrover into four-wheel drive or low reduction as the most exciting thing that could happen to Fiff all day, though she hadn't the vaguest idea what it was all about. The low-reduction lever was a kind of magic wand that enabled the Landrover to perform miracles of traction and stability.

"Four-wheel drive, dear!" she'd say whenever we came to a rough enough stretch of road for it to be even remotely necessary.

And if I was in the mood for it I'd make a great display of having to use the four-wheel drive and spin the steering wheel urgently back and forth to make it look right. Crossing open country would have her bobbing up and down on the seat like a wallaby in a rabbit trap.

"Low reduction, dear," she'd say, when I spun the wheels through a wet patch on purpose. "Make us go through there, dear. Be careful! There's a nice place! I wonder if we'll have to go up that bank through all the long grass by that log?"

And crossing a river or creek where the fan-belt had to be taken off and water came in the doors was something she'd still be talking about when we got to wherever we were going.

The Landrover was our only really important possession and I was careful not to knock it around too much and kept it in pretty fair condition. I carried plenty of spare everythings I could think of and every new part I put in it was an addition, as far as Fiff was concerned, not a replacement. God knows what would have happened if we'd had an accident and written the thing off. All the insurance companies in the world couldn't compensate Fiff for the loss of our Landrover. It was a bit of a worry.

Darcy dozed under the blitz and Fiff and I went for a swim in the ford with no clothes on. I kept teasing her that Darcy was coming and she'd squeal and try to hold hands in front of her $33\frac{1}{2}$-24–33 all at once. She's as funny as a cartload of monkeys when she's embarrassed.

The tide stayed in all day and Darcy woke up for long enough to explain that in the Gulf the tide could stay in or out for days because of the wind and the shallowness of the water. He'd seen three high tides in the McArthur in one afternoon. So we waited.

After a feed that night, Fiff and I crawled into our swag, tired from swimming, while Darcy went on watch to keep an eye on the tide. He woke us up about midnight. The river was low enough to sneak across if we were careful, but it had started rising again so we'd have to hurry.

We drove across without anything worse happening than our feet getting wet, and camped again on the other side. Darcy said that Yaloginda would have to wait for daylight so it might as well wait for us too, and he went to sleep on top of his swag with the mosquito net over him.

We arrived triumphantly in Yaloginda next day and dumped our bags of croc-skins at the store to be sent away.

"Everybody will be saying, 'here's the croc-shooters'," said Fiff.

We drove along to the pub. There's nothing else to do in Yaloginda except drive along to the pub, or away from it. That's what any croc-shooters would have done after a successful trip, so we didn't mind there being nothing else to do.

We ordered cans of beer and stood at the bar drinking and yarning about crocs as though we'd been at it all our lives. Fiff kept calling us lizard-skinners till I whispered for her to cut it out.

We'd got over sixty croc-skins on a very short trip, in time as well as distance. You could tell Darcy was pleased with the results, and us, by the way he told everyone about both.

Fiff went along to the little post office to post some letters she'd written and asked Darcy if he had any she could post for him. That was when he told us he didn't know whether he had any relatives left or not.

5

The Yaloginda Pub

I'D BEEN THINKING it might be about time for us to
have a go at some of Darcy's "big blokes", but he
hadn't said anything about us going out on
another trip with him and I didn't like to broach the
subject. He would probably say we were welcome
because of his being so polite, and I didn't want to
take advantage of his good nature. Fiff was thinking
about it too; I could tell by one or two things she
said. I decided to wait till I'd had a yarn with her
about it before asking Darcy, and put the matter
aside for the time being.

We drank all morning and had lunch at the pub.
Then we drank on and had dinner there. Although
Fiff wasn't drinking much she was getting very weary
and the party was getting a bit boisterous. A crowd of
ringers from a cattle-run were having the time of
their lives. I decided to take Fiff away and camp
somewhere.

When Darcy finished a foreign song he was singing

71

over and over I told him Fiff and I were going to camp down for the night. He seemed genuinely sorry we were going and carefully drew a map on the bar with a finger dipped in beer, showing us a good place to camp, on the bank of the Manara River, up from the bridge three miles out of town. We could drive right up to it and no one would disturb us there. He didn't know where he was going that night or what he was doing, but he'd meet us in the pub next morning at six o'clock. I told him it was a bit early and he said that was all right, he'd wait right there in the bar for us, even if we took all day. He seemed most anxious for us to come and I had to tell him several times we'd definitely be there. He came out to the Landrover with us and we all shook hands, thanked each other for something or other and Fiff and I hopped in and drove away. Pruszkowic came from under the blitz to help Darcy see us off. It was as sad as a parting.

We couldn't find the exact spot Darcy had described for us, but we found one that looked just as good. We cuddled and talked till we went to sleep. I dreamed about crocodiles and talked in my sleep, according to Fiff, who woke me up early next morning because she was lonely.

Darcy's blitz was parked under some trees about a hundred yards away with a tarpaulin and the harpoon-rope trailing over one side. We lit a fire and cooked something for breakfast. Pruszkowic came over to say good morning and Fiff suggested seeing Darcy about having us back. I said we'd never left him and she said I knew what she meant, and if I didn't she was going straight over to ask him herself.

So I poured a pannikin of tea for Darcy and wandered over to have a yarn with him. I told Fiff to stay behind because she might spoil it. She was full of advice about what to say to him but I didn't take any notice. You'd think a joker was going to fight him or something.

Darcy was sitting up in his swag against a wheel of the blitz. He didn't look too bright on it but he was glad of the brew of tea. We talked around for a while and then I asked him if there was any chance of me borrowing his harpoon-quill for the bloke at the garage to make me one the same. He said he had a spare one I could have and wanted to find it for me right there and then, but I told him there was no hurry.

Then I asked him if he knew where I could get a dinghy like his and he said it was very hard to get dinghies round there. We talked around some more and I asked him where was the best place to get on to the big blokes. He said that some of the biggest, cunningest old crocs in the Gulf were living further up the very river we were camped on. He'd been thinking of having a go at them himself for quite a while.

Of course I told him I wouldn't dream of going anywhere where he wanted to shoot himself and he said, no, I'd thought of it first and he wouldn't interfere with my river. The only thing for us to do, he reckoned, was to share my river and his boat.

"It is better for two men to handle those big blokes anyway. We will have to go fifty-fifty per cent in the supplies and the skins we will get, and work the Manara both together."

I pretended to think it over very carefully for a couple of seconds before I agreed. Darcy had to wait around Yaloginda for a day or two because he was expecting word about something. He wanted to get some stuffers stuffed to send up to the annual race meeting at Gregory in a week or so, and if Fiff was still interested he'd be pleased to teach her how to do them. I said I'd let her know.

Pruszkowic came back with me to tell Fiff, as though he'd arranged the whole thing. I told her how I'd put it straight to Darcy and he'd begged us to help him out on a trip up the Manara. And how I'd demanded half the skin-money we got. (That was to teach her a lesson for doubting I was game to ask Darcy in the first place.)

"I made him stick to his promise about teaching you how to do the stuffers, too," I told her, "He's doing some later to show you."

I wished that dog of Darcy's hadn't been there, though. I felt a bit silly about telling lies in front of him after he'd heard what really happened. He was disconcerting at times, the way he looked at a man — or perhaps it was just my guilty conscience.

Fiff was worried that I might have offended Darcy at first, but when he came over for something to eat you could see he was anything but offended. We talked about our trip up the Manara for a while and then Darcy and I drove into Yaloginda to see if the word he was waiting for had arrived yet.

In the bar of the pub there was a dirty big groper someone had caught in the river. They'd brought it into the pub to show everyone and it was still there because nobody knew quite what to do with it. It was easily the biggest fish like that I'd ever seen. It weighed over two hundred pounds and by the time Darcy and I walked in it was beginning to smell like it. It lay wetly in the middle of the floor with a black cloud of flies around it and a smell almost as tangible. The publican said he'd arranged for Stoneball Jackson to take it away somewhere but he hadn't got round to it yet.

Stoneball Jackson was an old prospector who pensioned himself off on the Miners' Sustenance every now and again for a spell in "The Smoke", as he called Yaloginda. When he'd had his spell he'd take to the hills again for a year or so. It was said he'd found enough rich strikes to keep him in luxury for the rest of his life, but he was happier the way he was, and sat on them. He was always talking about providing for his old age, but seeing that he was over sixty already it didn't ring terribly true. He was a bit of a nuisance at times, accidentally drinking your beer or picking fights with people half his age and twice his size, but you couldn't help liking him. He lived in the shell of a burnt-out car in a patch of scrub half a mile from the pub, when he was in town, and he had stakes driven in all along the track in case he got lost on his way to the pub in the mornings.

He was two hours later than usual this particular morning and when he did arrive you could see he'd been waiting for the price of shifting the groper to go up. It was doing that every minute, if the smell was any indication.

"When are you going to take that fish out of here, Stoneball?" the publican asked him.

Stoneball Jackson lifted a couple of empty beer cans and shook them to see if there was anything left and said, "Give us a can on the cuff, will you boss?"

"What about that fish?" asked the publican.

"What about that can?" asked Stoneball Jackson patiently.

The publican opened a can and banged it down on the bar in front of him. "Now, when are you going to shift that fish?" he demanded.

Stoneball Jackson took a long pull of his can and turned to look at the groper on the floor.

"Gettin' a bit ripe," he observed.

"I know it's getting bloody ripe," said the publican. "You were supposed to shift it out of here yesterday. I already paid you thirty bob for doing it."

"Yeah, I know," said Stoneball Jackson, drinking from his can again. "I was thinking you drove a hard bargain there, boss, expecting a man to shift a stinkin' thing like that for a lousy thirty bob."

The publican was getting a bit worried.

"Look, Stoneball," he said, "are you going to shift that thing or aren't you? You know bloody well it wasn't stinking when I paid you to shift it."

"Yeah, that's right," said Stoneball Jackson. "But we never made any allowance for me having to find somewhere to put it. That all takes time — and money."

"Throw it in the river, bury it, burn it. I don't care what you do with it," said the publican, "just so long as you get it out of here like you promised. It's your job to find somewhere to put it."

"I *have* found somewhere to put it," explained Stoneball Jackson patiently. "But while I've been arranging that end of it the job's got a little more difficult." He kicked the groper lightly with his boot and an angry buzz of flies swarmed up around him and the publican pulled a face, "I reckon you couldn't get a man to shift that thing for under three quid the way it is now. It's going to present difficulties," he added solemnly.

The publican agreed to pay the money in the finish, cursing Stoneball Jackson for a thieving old bastard. Stoneball fetched a tarpaulin, spread it out on the floor, rolled the leaking, dripping brown carcass of the groper on to it and dragged it out the door.

"Wouldn't have lasted much longer," he said innocently.

We went outside to see what he was going to do with it. He dragged it up the road to the police sergeant's place and rolled it off the tarpaulin in the garden. Then he came back and threw the tarpaulin back on Darcy's blitz. He offered to wash the floor of the bar down for ten bob, but the publican seemed to think he'd been used up quite enough for one day and did the job himself.

Half an hour later a message came that Stoneball Jackson was wanted over at the sergeant's place, right away. We watched poor Stoneball from the pub window, digging the dead groper into the sergeant's garden. It took him over an hour to get it all hacked up and buried. The publican was in fits of delight. Stoneball Jackson had outwitted himself at last! But Stoneball Jackson didn't look very outwitted when he came back into the bar. He got a can of beer and settled down with a satisfied look on his face.

"You fell in that time, didn't you?" laughed the publican.

"Fell in?" said Stoneball Jackson. "How do you mean?"

"We saw you burying that groper in the sergeant's garden," scoffed the publican. "You should have taken my advice and thrown it in the river."

"Like hell," said Stoneball Jackson. "I sold that groper to the sergeant yesterday for ten bob, for manure for his pumpkins. I left it till it was a bit ripe before I took it over so's I'd get the job of diggin' it in. Quid an hour he paid me — have a look!" and he produced the money to prove it.

Darcy was so entertained he didn't even go crook about his tarpaulin, which was in a hell of a mess. It was a torn old thing anyway. He threw it behind the pub because it was stinking up the gear on his blitz, and Stoneball Jackson washed it in the river and cut himself a new swag-cover out of it. Having a lot of money would take all the fun out of life for a man like Stoneball Jackson.

A couple of days later I saw the publican lend him a fiver because he was running a bit low on ready cash. They were good mates really and the constant blues they were having took the place of friendly gossiping, and was far more fun.

The word Darcy was waiting for hadn't come by half-past two in the afternoon, though he didn't go near the post office or check up with anyone, so I drove back to the camp on the river bank to see if Fiff was all right. She had a good fire going against a low bank and was baking loaves of camp-oven bread and boiling our dirty clothes. She was so busy I wished I'd stayed at the pub with Darcy, but I did a bit of work on the Landrover instead. The blitz bounced up drunk just after dark and Darcy nearly fell into the fire, and then into the river. I rolled him into his swag and left Pruszkowic to keep an eye on him. Fiff and I talked till very late and woke up bad-tempered too early next morning.

That was a hell of a day. The water in the river was salty and fresh water had to be carted from Yaloginda in drums. Fiff wanted us to get a load of water because she'd used nearly all we had doing the washing the day before, and I didn't want to. We drove into town in tempers (Darcy was too hangovery to get up yet) and had a hell of a row about something or other. She got out to walk in the finish and I said I was shooting through to Normanton and headed off with skidding wheels along the Normanton road.

I decided I didn't have enough petrol to get me to Normanton then, so I drove over to an old blackfellow's humpy out on the plain and brought a six-weeks-old dingo pup, swarming with ticks, from him. He was a Jolliffe-looking bloke and as crafty as they come. We bargained and argued for about half an hour and the price went from five bob to two quid and back again. Eventually I gave him his two quid and tore back to Yaloginda, flat out in case Fiff thought I'd really gone to Normanton and chased off after me.

She was talking to the cop's wife outside the store, so I drove slowly past looking the other way and wondering how to get rid of the pup. There was no need for it any more. It was a good chance to go to the pub anyway.

No one around the pub wanted a dingo pup covered with ticks so I took it back to Fiff and she sat in the hot shade under the store building picking the ticks off it. To hell with hanging around there, so I snarled at Fiff a bit and went back to the pub. Darcy wasn't there and Stoneball Jackson wasn't very entertaining, but I stuck it out for a couple of hours and then went back to be nice to Fiff. At the store they said she'd walked off down the road with a pup under her arm.

I flew into a bit of a panic. Some well-meaning idiot who didn't know any better had probably picked her up and taken her right through to Normanton. She was just in the mood to do it too. So back to the pub, drag the bloke out of the bar to open up his garage. Fill the Landrover with gas, top up the spare drum, and flat-out after the old dragon.

She had no right to go charging off like that without telling a man. I'd told *her* when I was going to Normanton — what's the big attraction there, anyway. Couldn't she think of a place of her own to run away to? She'd probably picked up the swag from the camp on her way past, too. I'd teach her to leave a man with no swag to sleep in!

I hit the Manara River bridge approach a bit on the fast side and nearly hit the rail. There she was, sitting on the bridge fishing. My good fishing-line, too. Not much use going crook at her, though. Then she had the cheek to go crook at me; for smacking the new pup for trying to pinch her bait. (She'll make a thief out of the flaming thing. Have to get rid of it. It's only going to be a nuisance.)

I took Fiff back to the camp and pretended I was going to leave her there while I went back to the pub. When we walked into the bar the garage bloke went a bit snotty about me not having to go to Normanton urgently after all and wasting all the trouble he'd gone to. We only stayed for one drink and then went back to camp to have a yarn with Darcy.

On the way out to the river I could see Fiff grinning at me. I drove on for a while not noticing and then turned round to call her a Cheshire bitch, but I grinned by accident and ruined it.

Darcy got up for a feed. We opened two cans of beef and sat round the fire talking till it got dark. I sat there yarning with Darcy for a couple of hours after Fiff hit the swag and when I crawled under the net she mumbled something about not fooling her one little bit. I didn't know what the hell she was talking about. I was going to tell her not to be so stupid, but it's one of our rules that no one's allowed to go crook after we're in bed at night. So I put her head on the right place on my shoulder and lay there listening to the river noises fading away in the darkness beyond the fire. What a crazy day. That's what happens when you've got nothing to do but wait around. (Hope the word Darcy's waiting for comes tomorrow.)

Next morning Darcy and I went into town again to see if his word had arrived yet and found quite a crowd of people there. A travelling carnival had arrived, on the back of a five-ton truck. The main attraction seemed to be a boxer who would take all corners for a fiver a time. The rest of the show appeared to be nothing but stands where they sold sweets and soft drinks and things. Honest, it wasn't much of an outfit, that's literally all there was of it; but for Yaloginda it was quite an event. It was going to start at eight o'clock that night and there was quite a crowd in the bar getting ready for it.

The boxer and the boss of the "carnival" were spouting about what a great show they were going to put on and shouting themselves beer lavishly. The boxer looked like a real thug. He was trying to jack up someone to fight him that night, but he was having a hard time even getting anyone to talk to him.

They looked like a couple of spruikers to me. Stoneball Jackson offered to fight the pair of them there and then but they just laughed at him and called him "Pop" and "Grand-dad", so he swiped the boxer's can of beer and retired to the far end of the bar to tell everyone what a gutless pair of dingoes they were.

Darcy and I had a can or two each and then drove back to camp in the Landrover to get Fiff. The way Darcy described the show to Fiff was a bit misleading and we had to wait out of sight for nearly a hour while she chose a dress and face-gear to wear to what she was determined to think of as a circus.

When we drove back into town there was a faded striped tent flapping limply beside the carnival truck on a section between the pub and the store, and shelves of coloured boxes of chocolates and sweets and things were being set up on the tray of the truck.

("Where's all the animals?" said Fiff.) We went into the bar, where we found that the main part of the show was over. Stoneball Jackson had clobbered the boxer bloke with a bar-stool and broken his nose and split his eyebrow. The boxing spectacle was off, but "the rest of the show would be going on just the same". The greatest selection of sweets, chocolates, soft drinks, balloons, lollies, whistles, dolls, candy, toys, and chewing-gum ever to hit Yaloginda would be on sale in the big-top at eight o'clock sharp!

Stoneball Jackson was asleep on the floor with his head propped up on a beer can and a borrowed hat to keep the noise out of his eyes. (He used to say that the racket of a crowded bar was better than a lullaby.)

We waited around for the carnival to start because of all the trouble Fiff had gone to getting ready and then bought a few bags of lollies. Darcy bought Fiff a whistle that unrolled when you blew it and an out-of-season Easter egg. Then we went back to camp because fights were starting outside the pub. Fiff put on a big billy of strong tea to take the taste of the carnival out of our mouths and we hit the sack early.

Darcy was restless that night. He came and squatted talking for hours outside our mosquito net. Fiff carried on sleeping but I sat up and asked him if it was not true about big crocs dragging horses and cattle into rivers and drowning them for food.

"Some of the big blokes drag cattle and horses into the rivers," he said. "Sometimes far more than themselves they can eat. They just leave them to float around for the other crocs to eat from and wait for the cattle to arrive back to drink again."

"But don't the cattle know there's crocs in the river?"

"Yes, the cattle they know about crocs, but in this country it is often fifty miles between waterholes and many cattle must drink from the brackish river water. That is where the croc waits. There are not many places where the cattle can get easily to the water because of the steep banks, you understand? Once they start drinking they tread on the mud and make the water dirty. So they crowd out into the clear water till they are up to their bellies. Cattle like to wallow — the old croc has many opportunities."

"But how do the crocs get hold of the cattle, Darcy?"

"They just move slowly up to the one they have chosen and suddenly snatch sideways at it. Then they sink with its head in their jaws. The weight of the croc is more than the cattle can pull away from and it is drowned."

"What about pigs and things like that, Darcy?"

"The croc can kill a pig or wallaby by crushing with his teeth," said Darcy. "I once found where a croc had stolen a boar pig from the mud among some man-groves in an estuary. The strength of the croc's jaw had broken the pig's stomach all over the trees around."

"Hell! How do they catch a wallaby?"

"I once saw a twelve-foot croc watching a wallaby hopping along the river bank. When the wallaby was some yards away the croc shouted loudly and ran and wriggled across to it, faster than any man could run. The wallaby was so surprised he forgot to run away. The croc snatched him and took him into the river very fast. There was much blood on the grass and other stuff."

"How big is a croc before he becomes a maneater?" I asked.

"Not all big crocs are maneaters. Also they are not all cattlekillers. Cattle and horses have only arrived in most of this country in the lifetime of one big bloke. And no crocodile lives only on men, although some very old ones will sometimes tip over a canoe to get at the people because they cannot get food in easier ways. Some of the biggest crocs I have killed have been slow and stupid, living just on mud-crabs and fish in estuaries along the coast. But if a croc has to get rough to make a living he is very prepared and able to do it, otherwise he is happy to live quietly.

"Do they have to have salty water to live in, Darcy?"

"No. A croc is very versatile. What is probably the reason for their survival. I have found quite a big salty seven miles from any water at all. And others in freshwater lagoons many miles from the sea or a river. When these waterholes begin to dry up the crocs will travel many miles to another place where there is more water, over country where a man would die of thirst or get lost. They have often been seen swimming far out to sea. They live on islands and beaches and in swamps and creeks and rivers, wherever there is food and water and warmth for them."

Darcy was just a natural encyclopaedia. He even talked like one when we got him going.

"Have they got any natural enemies?"

"Not once they grow to be big," Darcy replied.

"The one big enemy of the crocodile is the croc-shooter, and that is only very recently. After the hunter the real enemy of the croc is not the rifle or the net, or the snare or poison or old age, but the little spotlight. You will catch a few crocs by sneaking along the banks with your rifle, but only the spotlight is a match for the cunning of an educated crocodile. Until the croc-shooter with his spotlight came along there were many hungry crocodiles in the rivers and lagoons. And since the light has done what time has failed to do and had reduced their numbers to what they are, then there should now be plenty of food left for the remaining ones. The croc should therefore be not so dangerous to stock and swimmers as the same croc was fifty years ago."

He went on and on, for hours, about crocodiles. About the unaccountable mystery of their appearances and disappearances in rivers. How one night a big bloke you've been after for months will swim up to the light as though it's his turn for the harpoon. And the unexplainable something that tells an apparently sleeping croc that he's been sneaked up on.

"A croc is a coward when he is attacked and fearless when he is attacking. I have never known a croc to make an unpremeditated attack but I have known of many times when a croc has watched for days or weeks before he attacks."

"Perhaps they are not hungry at first?" I suggested.

"Many crocodiles with full bellies I have shot while they are trying to sneak up on a dog or a wallaby in the water. The croc has a liking for dogs. The croc will let a wallaby go and will take a dog every time. A dog of mine was holding a pig in shallow water at the edge of a river and he was taken by this croc. It carried my dog across the river and climbed out on to the mudbank and broke it up with its teeth and ate it. That was in a branch river that I don't think has ever been shot before. The crocs there were so cheeky that after my dog was stolen I moved my camp to a hill half a mile away from the river."

"Do they come out on the banks in the daytime much, Darcy?"

"While the water is warm the crocs will stay in it much of the time, but when the water runs cool in winter they lie out on the bank — sometimes. Nothing is certain except the uncertainty."

"What is the biggest croc you've every got, Darcy?"

"I have killed many thousands of crocodiles," said Darcy, "but never one over eighteen feet long. I believe that they grow to twenty feet long, and more, but fifty or sixty eighteen-footers is all I can say I have killed." He was actually apologetic as he said this. "But I am dreaming always that one day I will be killing a twenty-footer."

"How old do they grow to?" I asked.

"I do not know, but I think some of the really old ones are more than a hundred years. There are many arguments about this."

"Would they make good pets?"

"No, they do not make pets, even bad ones. No man can really learn to know a croc because we can only compare the way they behave with the way people behave, and there is no comparison. A dog is aggressive or cowardly; a bird is timorous; a fish is nervous, a boar is brave and will stand and fight when he is attacked; a rat is sneaky. All these things we can understand. We can even say of a shark that it is a moving appetite and that is the nearest thing to a crocodile I can think of as far as the behaviour concerned. But no man ever made a friend of a crocodile. You can take one from the egg, feed it and keep it happy for all your life. Then it will kill you because it is a crocodile, and crocodiles and men are more different than hot and cold. It is the difference of millions of years. The crocodile has been overlooked by time."

Daylight was sneaking through the trees when Darcy rose and walked stiffly through the lifting shadows to his lonely bed. I wouldn't have missed that talk at any price. Sleep can be caught up on, but a man like Darcy in a mood like that is a rare thing.

There were things he told me about crocodiles that I never proved for myself, but I never discovered anything on which he was wrong, even his theories. According to a book Fiff wrote away for, all they know about crocs is that they are the bulkiest of all living reptiles, grow from sixteen to thirty feet long and have been hanging around for well over a hundred million years without changing their shape, style of living, or their stamping-grounds much. About the crocodiles as they are today I think Darcy knew a lot more than any book could have told us.

At that stage I hadn't even seen a saltwater crocodile, but Darcy's reports and comments were as convincing as the cow I was to see later, standing hopelessly out on the plain with its bottom jaw torn away.

6

Crocs and Stuffers

I T WAS LATE in the morning when we got up for breakfast. Darcy and I went off to the pub to see if his word had arrived yet and to pick up the blitz. We'd left it there the night before and Darcy had come home in the Landrover.

When we got to the pub the carnival was gone and so was the blitz. There was a message for Darcy that his friend on a station had taken the loan of it for a day or two, so it was all right. Except that all our croc-shooting gear was on the back of it and Pruszkowic had nothing to sit under and guard. The Landrover was too low to the ground for him.

I was anxious to get after those big blokes up the Manara River and over a can of beer I asked Darcy exactly what was this "word" he was waiting for.

"Word to make another trip," he said, patting his pocket significantly. "When this is empty I am ready to go and get some more croc-skins. I prefer to be a poor croc-shooter than a rich man with no work.

This way I have no boss to say: 'Darcy, you must do this work or I shall send you to look for a new job, where the boss will say, 'Darcy, you must do this work. . . . ' "

I got the point.

Darcy and I drank quite a lot of beer that day. In fact, it was a hell of a lot. Around dark I left Darcy enjoying himself in the pub and drove back to the camp to give a bit of cheek to Fiff. I fell out of the Landrover, staggered across, and passed out at her feet. With a hole in my pants, so she reckoned.

Next morning I heard strange voices and opened one eye to have a look. I saw that I was the only one left in the swag. Another waggon was parked beside ours and two prospectors who'd brought Darcy home the night before were eating damper round a bottle of O.P. rum on the bonnet. When I got up I found that they were Bob, the old bloke, and Dick, who was only a young bloke like me. Darcy was crooker than I was, and I'd been seen in much better condition than I was then.

Bob was a typical old prospector. He had the usual kind of prospecting yarns that everybody likes listening to. He'd discovered a pretty terrific copper show a few years back, but some big mining company had found something wrong with the way his claim was registered and moved in without paying him a cracker. The court case was still coming up. He could track like a blackfellow and he'd done time in Fanny Bay for cattle-duffing when he was a young bloke. And he drank O.P. rum out of the bottle as though it was ordinary petrol, without turning a hair.

Dick was a quiet sort of bloke, but friendly enough.

He blushed whenever Fiff looked at him and whenever she didn't. When she spoke to him he'd stammer and shuffle his feet in the dirt. Poor sod.

Fiff wanted to go out to the big saltpan beyond Yaloginda to see some mirages we'd been hearing about. Bob wasn't interested in mirages and Darcy was still too crook to be interested in anything so they stayed behind. Me, Fiff and Dick crowded into the Landrover and went off to see the mirages.

We saw them all right, but there wasn't much to see. Just black lines of trees and hills lifted a few feet off the horizon and trembling in waves of heat. Fiff was quite indignant and said how mirages should be right up in the sky and only when you're dying of thirst. But we saw a dingo sliding furtively through the Mitchell grass. And three graceful big dancing birds that stood five feet high and in a row and bounced out of step for us as light as balloons, till Fiff started clapping and frightened them into dancing away across the saltpan as though they were caught in a strong wind. Dick shot a wallaby with the .222 for meat for Pruszkowic. It was a pleasant afternoon. That night we all planned to get away to other camps next day. We hit the sack early and sober for a change.

In the morning we packed up our gear but couldn't get away, so all the men went to the pub instead. At the pub there was a message saying Darcy's blitz would be back there tomorrow morning and we decided to go up the river next day by road and across country and set up a camp to work from. Action at last! That night we took some beer back to the camp for a big break-up party, but Fiff didn't feel

93

like it, Darcy had already had enough, I was too sick, and Dick was already asleep. So Bob had to have a party on his own, which he made quite a tidy little job of. The man was undrunkable.

Next morning we said goodbye all round and drove off in opposite directions.

When we reached Yaloginda Darcy found something to be really outraged about. The blitz was there all right, but his gear was in such a mess it was going to take him a full day to find out what was missing and what was only broken. Our little dinghy was split along one side where it had landed on something.

Fiff and I waited silently for the blast while Darcy surveyed the mixture. He picked an axe off the tray of the blitz, looked at the split handle for a moment and then put it gently back again.

"The man has been very careless," he said.

"Where is he?" I asked. "We'll make the bastard fix this up!"

"No," said Darcy, shaking his head. "One day this man will want again to borrow something from me or ask for my help. Then he will regret his lack of respect for my property."

We bought fuel and supplies and drove off across the plain on the road along which Fiff and I first came to Yaloginda. About fifteen miles out we turned off on a set of wheel-tracks that took us back towards the Manara River. On a grassy bank above the river Fiff and I set out a camp while Darcy patiently began to sort through his gear. He was still at it by dark.

Next morning he and I crossed the river in the badly-leaking dinghy and set off along the opposite bank upstream, looking for signs of crocs. We had the

.222, bare feet, shorts, knives and Pruszkowic. And were on the wrong side of the river. Three times we heard the sudden rushing splash from under the bank we were walking along, but we were too close to the crocs to see them. If we'd been across the river we'd at least have had a chance to look across to them. The vegetation on the twenty-foot bank between us and the mass of reeds at the water's edge made it impossible for us to see them.

Where the first croc went splashing in beneath us we followed a wallaby-track down through the scrub and found a private little beach with scattered bones. A wet slide where the "big bloke" had gone into the water gave me a thrill to guess at his size. At least eighteen feet!

"Hell, Darcy," I whispered, "He's a big bloke!"

Darcy, glancing at the slide, nodded and said, "Yes, about twelve feet long."

Darcy was good at telling tracks, from having lived among the blacks. He could tell at a glance things you'd never guess were possible to learn from marks on the ground. And he'd explain the how and why of them, too. It was much more impressive than any inscrutable-faced inch-by-inch examination and taciturn diagnosis could ever have been.

I'd been standing well back from the water on the croc's little beach out of respect for the size of that slide, even though it was only made by a twelvefooter. Darcy leaned the rifle against the bank, walked out through the reeds, dived in and swam a few strokes out into the river. I grabbed the rifle, sure that he'd gone stark staring mad.

"What the hell are you doing?" I shouted.

"Washing the sweat off myself so I won't be so easily smelt by crocs further along," he replied. "Come and wash yourself."

"What about the crocs?"

"This is one time he will not touch us. It is too sudden for him. He will have to think about us before he makes up his mind. When he decided we will be gone already. Come into the water. It's quite safe."

I dived recklessly into the shallows among the reeds and sprang back out as though I was on the end of a big rubber band. To hell with that caper.

The next croc we disturbed went into the river with a great slopping surge and Darcy ran to peer through a gap in the branches because sometimes they dive in and come straight up again for a look. This one didn't. We went down and found a perfect curving imprint of an *enormous* croc. Surely this one was well over eighteen feet long!

'Fifteen-footer," said Darcy.

"But look how wide it is! See the size of those claw marks!"

"Yes, Once they get to reach twelve or thirteen feet they grow thicker for their length."

"But look at the width of it!"

"Yes," repeated Darcy patiently. "About fifteen feet."

The next croc we heard was a mere eight- or ten-footer. And that was all we saw that day — or I should say heard, because we didn't actually see any of them. On the way back Darcy said that to see evidence of that many was a probable indication there were at least twice as many in that stretch of the river, about two and a half miles.

"They always lie on a bank with their heads turned towards the water like that," explained Darcy. "And these big blokes are never far from deep river. They're uneasy in shallow places. If one moves off in a definite direction when you put the light on him, you can say to yourself that this croc is going to deep water. When he stops or turns around you can say to yourself, here is where he feels safe. It is the deepest part around here, or the safest in some other way. Then you can prepare to use your harpoon, for it is then that he will let you come close to him if he is going to.

"It doesn't always happen this way, only often enough to be often. There are so many things to know and be prepared for. The water, the current, the season, the place, the crocodile — I cannot tell a man all these things. Now when my light falls on a crocodile I can say: 'This crocodile is mine, but I must be very patient with him'; or 'Here is a stupid crocodile who will wait for me to kill him.' Or sometimes I say: 'This crocodile will go down many times and move around beneath the water. Only if I am very lucky will I get this one.' Very often I am wrong. There is much to learn."

"What about the seasons, Darcy? What difference do they make to the croc-shooting?"

But Darcy had said enough about crocs for one day. "You will learn that as the seasons pass," he said. "If you want to learn about crocodiles you must try to comprehend a little of what you see now and let the experience help you understand what you see later. The seasons will come much faster than knowledge. . . . There is a dust-storm coming."

There was too. A haze in the middle distance that didn't seem to get any closer, till I realised my teeth were gritting on an almost invisible dust that hung in the air, almost transparent. We cut a new harpoon-pole and by the time we got back to the camp the dust was in our very bones. The dust-storm hung in the red air for three days, till there came a wind from out in the Gulf to take it away again.

The water in the river at our camp was not so salty as it had been further down, but it was still far from drinkable. So next day I drove into Yaloginda to fill our drums while Darcy straightened out his gear and mended the dinghy.

While I was in town I dropped in to the pub for a beer. There was a travelling jeweller in the bar, all the way from Mount Isa. He had a big display of watches and knick-knacks set up on the bottom of an upside-down tea-chest. He was explaining to the only other customer the merits of a Railway-Lever. The customer was Stoneball Jackson with mischief in his eye. I didn't wait to see it. (I heard later that Stoneball bought one of the jeweller's waterproof watches and tested it by soaking it overnight in a mug of beer. Then he demanded his money back and asked the jeweller to fix the watch up for him.)

When I got back to camp with the water and one or two things for Fiff (she had to have them sent from Cairns because they didn't carry things like that at the Yaloginda store) Darcy's gear was more or less in order and the glued patch on the dinghy was drying in the sun. Darcy and Fiff were just about to begin her first lesson in stuffing little crocodiles. I never learned how to do it myself but I've seen Fiff do dozens of them. As far as I can make out, this is how Darcy's method goes. I can guarantee it, providing I give you the right instructions and you do them right.

From the time a croc comes out of the soft-shelled egg, hatched in the hot sand on a river bank, he's ready to go into business. Just as voracious as his old man, only on a smaller scale. Before he and his twenty-odd brothers and sisters reach the water there are likely to be only ten of them — kookaburras, dingoes, snakes and things, everything has a go at them. And when he gets into the river the sharks and other fish are after him. Even his old man is liable to scoff him if he gets in the way. He lives for a few days — or weeks — or months; or even a couple of years, popping up and down along the overgrown banks eating crabs, little fish, and things. Then one night Darcy comes whirling along in his dinghy and snatches him with a quick grab behind the neck and puts him in a cold wet sack, along with several of his brothers or sisters or cousins. By morning he is dead. (I wonder how many millions of years of potential life Darcy has interrupted?)

One slit up the stomach is the only opening in the skin. First skin the body — "Take the croc away from his skin, don't pull the skin off or you shall tear it," says Darcy. Then sleeve-skin the hind legs to the first knuckles of the claws, like peeling the stocking off the leg of a woman, only different, and cut them through at the soft white knuckles. Then do the tail (use your common sense). Work the skin off the body to where the brassiere would be if it was a woman. Then the same with the front legs as you did with the back ones, only leave out the rips and knife-cuts. (They don't really matter for a start.) Part the croc from the skin right up to the line of the jaw and base of the skull. Cut through the spine at the ball-joint behind the skull.

Now you're supposed to have a miniature croc-skin, with claws and head attached, and very little croc still on the inside of the skin, but don't worry — it happens to everybody the first few times. Scrape the skin carefully, dig out the brains and smother the whole inside of the skin, skull and legs with salt. Pack the whole thing with salt and then bury it in the salt bag along with all the other little croc-skins you've made a botch of. Oh yes, don't forget to dig the eyes out. Point of a knife.

After three or four days change the salt. At least three or four days later, and at the most three or four months, take the skin and wash all the salt out of it. While it's still soft, fill the legs with fine dry sawdust and ram it firm with a round stick. Get your needle and waxed thread and stitch the skin in a neat line from the end of the tail to the back legs. Stuff the tail the same as the legs. Then sew and stuff till you've got the whole thing packed like a gollywog, with the legs and tail straight and firm.

Now you've got to set it. Bend the legs and curl the tail till they look natural. Belly, tail and feet all touching the floor is best for the start (you can sit them up on their tail after you've got the knack). Lift the head and prop the jaws open. You'll have found that you have to block the throat with paper to stop the saw-dust running out again. By this time you'll have nails and blocks of wood all over the place holding the croc in your realistic position. You can put it out in the sun now. The sun dries and shrinks the skin round the sawdust packing.

After a few hours you can tell it's set properly because it won't be floppy any more. Open your tin of putty and cover the stitching along the belly and any of the knife-cuts you've had to patch up. Cover the paper wadding in the throat and smooth over the tongue. Marbles are good for the eyes — or beads — or berries, anything that won't rot. More sun and final adjustment till the putty dries.

Now you can get out the clear varnish and give the whole works a good coat, then another. When that dries you've got the finished article.

Even Darcy made a botch of his first few but now he could do eight-footers. He'd even do you an eighteen-footer if the price was right.

Darcy and Fiff did four stuffers that day, and another four the day after. And Darcy and I took them in to Yaloginda to leave at the pub to be taken to the races at Gregory.

The next day Darcy and I had to go to the pub again to give the stuffed crocs in the pub to a bloke in the pub to give to his brother in the Gregory pub whose mate was going to sell them for us. It was a pretty weak excuse and I felt a bit lousy about leaving Fiff out at the camp while Darcy and I were celebrating the day before the races at Gregory. Some blokes in a private plane called in on their way to Gregory, so I got them to drop a note in a weighted sack to Fiff at the camp on the river bank to cheer her up a bit. Then I went out there myself to get her in case they dropped the note in the river and she didn't get it. I had a good excuse ready for why I had to come back, but I didn't need it. So I saved it up. (Still haven't used it so I won't say what it was.)

When Fiff and I got back to the pub, Darcy was in great form. Someone had offered him the use of a fifteen-foot boat and outboard motor. All Darcy had to do was look after three dogs while the bloke was away at the races and bring him back two small live crocs. The live crocs were no trouble, but all those dogs were likely to be a bit of a nuisance.

That night Darcy was to bring the boat up the river to the camp. He took a spotlight and rifle and we took Pruszkowic, the dingo pup and the three snarling guests in the Landrover. I shot two wallabies for dog-tucker on the way and Fiff and I were on our own for the first time in weeks. It wasn't much of an evening though. The dogs howled and barked and Darcy arrived at about eleven o'clock. He'd shot a fourteen-foot croc just down-river from the camp. He would have got a bigger one as well but he hadn't taken the harpoon. I was jealous about not having been in on it.

In the morning we all went down to skin Darcy's fourteen-footer. It was in a hell of a place, in four feet of water because the tide was in. Darcy hopped into the water and felt around with his foot till he found the dead croc. Between us we managed to snig it up into a muddy washout, but its head was still under water. The thing was too big and heavy to take somewhere we could work on it properly. We had to skin it standing up to here in mud. A hell of a job, both of us working on it in awkward slippery restricted space. It took us two hours.

The difference between saltwater and freshwater crocs is not a big one. Apart from the size of it, the salty has a broader, more craggy head and jaws than the finer and scissor-like jaw-action of the freshy. Blunt and grinning, it was, and felt like smoother dark rock with boar-tusk teeth, the end ones sticking up through holes in the nose. The jaws fit raggedly but perfectly, like the serrated edge of a key, and you could lift open the top jaw and let it fall shut with a loud wooden clap. Rigor mortis takes a long time to set in in a dead croc. One of the first things you realise is how helpless a man would be once one of those things grabbed him. You wouldn't have a chance. The weight of the skin alone was as much as I could lift and carry through the clutching mud to Fiff in the dinghy.

Then Darcy did a post mortem to see what the dead croc had been eating. Bones, quite big ones, the pelvis of a wallaby — no, a dog! Here's a bit of the collar with the buckle and a rivet still on it. Leg bones. Pig bristles, balls of wallaby and cattle-dog hair. Four of them, the size of tennis balls. More bones. And rocks! Round ones, about a dozen, the size of your fist.

"What are the rocks for, Darcy?"

"Some people will tell you that the rocks in the stomach of a crocodile are to help him digest the bones and things he eats, but I am not believing this. I think the crocodile swallows rocks to balance his buoyancy, so he can lie on the bottom of the river without effort and stay on the surface by gently swimming. A croc doesn't dive when he goes down, you understand? He fades down, he sinks. The rocks in his stomach are to help him maintain the correct weight. You will see how only the top edge of his head appears at the surface of the water when he comes up to breathe or watch, while his body hangs down at an angle. Only when he is actually swimming along on top of the water does his back show above the surface."

Darcy showed me where to place the shots that will kill a big croc best. "Always in the head; body shots often only wound them and make holes in the skin. The ear, a slit in the side of the head two inches behind the eye, is a good place. A tunnel through the bone leads to his brain. Otherwise you must hit him flat and square and hope the bullet shatters the skull. A .303 at point-blank range will often fail to penetrate a croc's skull. Think of that! Have you seen what a .303 does to an axe-head?"

Most of the big skins have rips and holes in them from fighting. Darcy says that a ten- or twelve-footer is the best size for first-grade skins and the easiest to handle. They fight for sex, or to see who's boss in a section of the river, or for some other dark crocodily reason; Darcy is not prepared to say. He told us how he was watching a big croc swimming down a river one day. He couldn't shoot it then because the water was too deep so he'd decided to have a go at him with the light that night. He just sat there and watched it swimming along. Then another croc, about the same size — twelve or thirteen feet — came swimming along from the other direction.

Without even changing gear they swam up to one another, circled a couple of times and then it was on, chopping and grunting at each other as though it had been put on specially for Darcy's benefit. Then one of the crocs grabbed the other round the base of the tail and hung on. The other grabbed him at the side of the belly, and round and round they went, till Darcy fired a shot and broke up the fight because they were ruining good croc-skins. He got both of them that night. Two second-grade skins with big holes in them.

We fed the dogs when we got back to camp and let them off for a run. Then Darcy scraped and salted the croc-skins, while Fiff baked bread. I smoothed and trimmed our new harpoon-pole and dug a neat hole in the thick end with a sharpened screwdriver so the quill fitted firm and smooth into it. Then I bolted and bound the gaff on the other end. After that I took the liberty of cleaning up Darcy's rifles a bit and putting a drop of oil here and there. His .303 was shooting two inches low at twenty-five years. He said he knew about that and allowed for it, so I didn't alter the sights.

Darcy and I were going out after the big blokes that night.

7

Big Salty

I T WAS MID-AFTERNOON and steaming hot when Darcy and I left the camp in the little dinghy — paddling, because Darcy said we were better off doing a short section of the river properly than roaring along for miles in the big boat with the outboard motor, picking up the odd easy ones and disturbing everything else.

"You can quite often get up to an old croc with an outboard motor," he said, "but you must be careful not to change the speed of it, keep it at a steady sound and blind him with the light so he doesn't know how close you are coming. This theory is very good. Only I am not certain that the light does blind a croc. It doesn't stop them from swimming away in any direction if they want to. And it doesn't seem to make any difference how dull or bright the light is, so long as it lights up their eyes. It could be that it hypnotises the croc, when he is in some moods. I know this, though, I've lost many crocodiles using an outboard motor on my boat that I would have got if I'd been using my paddle. Too many disturbing noises. Stopping and starting the motor or putting it in and out of gear. The big space you need to manoeuvre the boat in. Driving the shooter into the branches overhanging the banks because you can't stop in time. Hitting logs under the water with the propeller. The smoke and the fumes drifting ahead of you, blinding your light, disturbing crocs you can't see further on. I can stop my little dinghy and turn it right round with one sweep of the paddle. [He could too!] I don't have to carry fuel and spare parts or learn how to fix a motor. And I can work on my own when I have no mate with me.

"The only real advantage of using an outboard motor is that it's easier and quicker. In the end it is only a matter of the time it takes to cover a river. I have plenty of time. I will get my crocodiles."

So we paddled up the river in the little dinghy, and it was very pleasant. The gently kiu-kiuing of pigeons in the overhanging tea-trees. Hushing of air through she-oaks, and rifle-fish, like spotted patches of shade, splashing along the reeds. Leaves and debris on the smooth water revolving slowly upstream on a filling tide. The dinghy slid along, in and out of the shade along one bank, under Darcy's lazy, easy paddling. The rising water gurgled loudly into holes in the mud at the banks, and around the second bend we met the coming and going stink of something dead a crocodile had hidden somewhere.

"Smell that?" I whispered.

He nodded.

"Croc?"

He nodded again.

"Do you think there's something dead around here?"

Darcy laid the paddle across the bow of the dinghy and began to roll one of his rare smokes.

"I have never seen where a croc has buried anything he's killed." he said. "But if he'd made a good job of it I would not have been able to. And they could not bury a cow or horse. Most of the things they kill are just left to be floating around till they're ready to eat. Wallabies and pigs are mostly dragged into the reeds, but anything that is left out in the current just floats up and down on the tides, you understand? It doesn't go far."

We carried on, and an hour later Darcy pointed with his paddle to a big wet slide running down a sloping bank in an isolated patch of mangroves.

"Slide," I whispered. 'Big salty!"

"Yes," said Darcy interestedly. "Big bloke."

He paddled across and swept the dinghy close in to the bank, holding it there with the paddle stuck in the mud. "About twelve or fourteen feet. We might see him later."

"How much farther are we going today, Darcy?"

"We shall paddle until the tide turns and then hunt crocs on the going-out tide back to our camp. It is important to know how your tides are working because they can help you, or make it hard for you, whichever you shall prefer. You have to learn that in some places it is better to go after your croc when the tide is low, because when the water is high he can hide from your light under the branches of the trees that reach into the water. In other places you must wait until the water is rising so you can float across bars and logs. Always go up a strange river in the daylight so you know what your light is shining on when you return in the dark looking for crocodiles."

An hour later the current on the river was still and it was high tide. We found a little beach among reeds and put ashore. There was about an hour and a half to wait before it would be properly dark, and we lit a small fire to boil up the water we'd brought for a brew of tea.

"As soon as it becomes dark we can begin searching for crocodiles," said Darcy. "It is as good a time of the night as any other."

"How much further does this river go, Darcy?"

"I remember it to fork a few miles further on. One branch is deep and narrow and runs back for many miles. It is very twisting, like all creeks that drain flat country. One moment the wind is behind you and then it blows in your face. In two miles you are only a few hundred yards in a straight line from the mouth. The other branch is wide and shallow and ends very soon in mangrove swamps and creeks and mud. There are crocodiles there but they are hard to get to. The mosquitoes and sandflies would kill a man if he was left in there for one night without fire."

We drank tea and talked and soon it was nearly dark and time for us to go. I packed the tea billy and pannikins into their sack with the plastic water-jar and fitted them under the seat in the stern of the dinghy. Then we checked the gear to be certain we'd brought everything. Harpoon, quill, and rope. Knife, headlight, and battery. Axe, smokes, croc-box, sacks folded on the seats for us and the rifles. Bailing-tin, sack for the stuffers. Ropes and mosquito repellent. And rifles.

"Everything's here."

I sat in the stern of the dinghy.

"All right. Let us start back. I am hoping for two crocodiles. We shall see."

He pushed us away from the bank and sat in the bow. Out in the stream he adjusted his light on his forehead and carefully lined it up with the .303 on a floating leaf. The boat began to slide along the river under the big silent strides of Darcy's paddle, the spotlight searching the river for the red eyes of the "big blokes".

I noticed Darcy's routine with the light. When he came round a bend he raked the light lightly over the whole stretch of water and any crocs that were there would usually be lit up at once. Even if he did spot one he would still give the rest of the place a good rake-over in case there were more crocs or a bigger one. Up and down along each bank several times, working forward with the progress of the dinghy.

Half an hour later the soundless dip and swirl of the paddle was interrupted as Darcy steered the dinghy towards a glimpse of red in some reeds on the bank ahead. Then suddenly he veered off towards the blazing wide-apart eyes of a big salty further down the river.

Never mind the little one in the reeds now. Here's a real big bloke!

Darcy paddled steadily down towards the glowing eyes at the end of the unwavering light and I was sure that here was my first big salty. I could hear my own jerky breathing. Suddenly a garfish came flashing in to the boat and fell riggling into the bailing-tin. I nearly yelled with fright and it was a second or two before I tipped the blasted thing over the side. The croc didn't move and Darcy paddled on as though he hadn't heard the fish.

Closer — the eyes vanish. Darcy stops paddling but lets the dinghy drift on. The croc might come up again — there he is further on. Keep going. Deep water here. A harpoon job.

Closer — pole in one hand, paddle in the other. He gently gathers in the slack rope along the pole from the fixed quill to his handhold. The ridged snout, and the thick neck just under the water behind the eyes. We're getting too close! Throw it, you fool! Now — oo! Got him!

The croc vanishes in a thrashing churn of water, but the rope looping out over the bow of the rocking dinghy tells he's fixed on the quill. Darcy picks the dropped pole out of the water and puts it quietly back in the boat. He picks up the knife, just in case.

The rope stops feeding out. There's still a few coils left between Darcy's feet. He picks up the .303 and closes the bolt on a cartridge. A gentle tug on the slack rope to get his position. The rest of it runs out and the dinghy is jerked half round.

Silence. The river is oil. Crabs crack and plop in the mangroves and mud-skippers flash silver like knife-blades against the mud in the sweeping light. The dinghy swings slackly across the current. He's got to come up for air. . . .

Suddenly red eyes out in the middle of the stream. The comfortable roar of the .303 and the great white belly floats in the light and begins to fade down-stream into the water.

Quick! Drag him in before he sinks. Loop the rope round his jaws. He's still twitching.

"Pass me the axe."

Chunk! chunk! behind the head. There, that's fixed him. Drag him across to the bank. Tie him to this tree with a piece of spare rope and cut out the harpoon-quill. Mark the place — break branches and leave them hanging.

"Remember that dead tree sticking out into the river? We shall come back and skin him tomorrow when the tide is out. About the same size as the other one we got, fourteen-footer. Skin should be worth about thirty quid if it's first grade. I didn't see any marks on it. We'll go back and have a look for that freshy we saw first when we've had a smoke."

"How many more do you think we'll get, Darcy?"

Darcy stopped coiling the stiff wet harpoon rope and looked at me blindingly with the light on his forehead. "If we don't get any more crocodiles tonight we have still done very well. You can paddle all night in a river like this and not see one."

The first croc was still there. Darcy drifted the dinghy up to it, shot it with the .22, chopped it behind the head and passed it back to me. A five-foot freshy.

We lit up another big bloke that went down and stayed there when we got to within fifty yards of him. Darcy switched off the light and we drifted in the dark for what seemed half an hour. Suddenly the light went on again with a quick sweep and found the eyes. Upstream, fifty yards. Twenty-five yards and down he

115

went again. Darcy drew the dinghy up to where the eyes went down, but he seemed to expect the croc to come up on the other side of the river. It did! Darcy shot him on the move and just managed to get the harpoon into him before he went out of sight, but Darcy fell into the river doing it. I nearly went after him attempting an alarmed and clumsy rescue and he had to tell me to get on the other side of the boat so he could climb back in without tipping it up. We found the harpoon-pole floating against the bank and then Darcy gently drew in the croc while I stood behind him ready with the .303. It was an eleven-footer, dead as a doornail. Darcy re-killed it with the axe and we laid it out in the dinghy.

There was another big bloke further down but Darcy didn't waste much time on him. The first glimpse of his eyes was the only one we got.

The camp was in darkness when we got back but those dogs made sure we didn't miss the place. Fiff got up to see what we'd got and put on a feed for us. It was two o'clock when we crawled into our swags, and seven in the morning when Pruszkowic woke us up barking at a seven-foot king-brown snake, fifteen yards from the camp. I blew its head off with the .222 and we got a photograph of Pruszkowic frowning disapprovingly at the dead coils beside the Landrover.

After a wallaby breakfast we skinned the two crocs we'd brought in the night before. Then we all went up the river to skin the big bloke we'd left tied to the tree. It was afternoon by the time we had the three skins salted and rolled up in a sack. Then we prepared our gear and ourselves for a trip to the head of the river next day. We would camp near the forks Darcy had spoken of and work from there. We didn't go out shooting that night.

Next morning we set off up the Manara in the big fifteen-foot boat with the outboard motor, towing the little dinghy because Darcy wouldn't hear of leaving it behind and it was handy to carry the dogs in. They would have been a hell of a nuisance climbing wet all over our gear. Pruszkowic was very indignant about not being allowed to ride in the front of the boat with the people, and the dingo pup kept climbing out and having to be gone back for.

On up the river, past where we'd got the first big bloke. The bloated carcass of a big cattle-beast floating high among some reeds.

"Must have been a big croc to drag that into the river and drown it?"

"They are not all dragged down and drowned and floated out by the tides. Cattle can fall down banks and fail to find a place where they can climb out. You are not to be blaming the croc for *every* death in the river; but most of the time it is he."

We saw five cattle and several wallabies floating in the river that day, and smelt several other dead somethings.

Round a bend we saw a great grey battleship of a croc slide smoothly into the water. Darcy said that he would have heard us coming from a long way back and waited to have a look at us. There was something contemptuous about the lazy way he sank into the water. We saw and smelt a horde of flying-foxes, hanging in the trees and wheeling thick and screeching in the air at our passing. Wallabies ran leaping from the shade and up over the banks and we had to shout at the dogs and throw floating sticks at them. A black pig trotted along a sand-bar with four little pigs in a tidy row behind it and disappeared into a thick tangle of dead scrub, as though it had been rehearsed. The horrified scrallings of white cockatoos in a tree leaning over the river.

Beyond the forks we found a good camping-place near fresh water and distant from rotting animals. It was a strange place to me and yet there was a familiar atmosphere about it. Must have been the missus being there.

Some of my favourite memories are of things that happened during our stay in the headwaters of the lazy Manara. We got a hoary old seventeen-footer by the forks on the first night we went out from that camp. It took the two of us all day to do the hide. It was heavier than one man could lift. We harpooned a wallaby swimming in the river ahead of an eleven-foot freshy. We wanted the wallaby for dog-tucker and Darcy could tell we were going to get the croc anyway. It was the biggest freshy he'd ever seen. Me too.

The dogs we were looking after were a bigger nuisance than the sandflies and mosquitoes. They were always fighting, pinching something, getting in the way, vanishing, or making a noise. They annoyed Pruszkowic as much as us. I'm afraid Fiff was their only friend.

We shot an eight-foot salty on a log and harpooned a one-eyed "rogue" in a side creek. (I've never been able to find out what exactly a rogue crocodile is, but there are plenty of them around. It sounds good.) We discovered a branch of the river that had never been shot before because we had to hack a path for the dinghy through overhanging branches to get into it.

"But there's no reason why we should believe that the crocs in this creek have never been hunted," said Darcy. "They move about from place to place and most of them will have been out in the main river often enough to get chased by outboard motors and experts with big hats and quick rifles. That may well be why they are in this creek. Otherwise the main river is a much better place for a crocodile to live."

I was beginning to realise what I was seeing when Darcy leaned forward in the dinghy with a croc lit up in his spotlight. His attention was fixed not so much on what he could see, but what he knew was there. Not interested in what the croc was doing, but what it was likely to do. If it stayed where it was it was as good as dead.

"When he goes down in a creek watch for him to come up at the opposite bank. In a big river he will come up again out in the middle. If he keeps going down and coming up further along the river he is heading for somewhere and won't let you come close to him until he is there and feels safe. These are not habits, just possibilities."

Darcy dived in eight feet of water for a dead croc. "If he was only wounded he would not be still here. I can feel him down there but I can't get the rope round him. Pass me the harpoon. I shall dive down and stab it into him and we shall try and raise him with it."

It worked.

I was learning how to paddle and sneak. One day I was paddling on my own up a creek with a can of water to hold the stern of the dinghy down when I saw the head and shoulders of quite a big croc resting on the bank ahead. I drifted the dinghy back out of sight and beached it round the corner on the opposite bank from the one the croc was on. Then I began to stalk along the bank with my .222, well back from the river and creeping up to peer over the bank every twenty or thirty yards. He was still there. I moved along a few feet and rested the rifle ever so slowly through a clump of Mitchell grass. It was an easy shot, but to make absolutely sure I took several sights through the 'scope before gently squeezing off a shot with the cross-bar dead-centre on the back of the skull where Darcy had shown me for this angle. The croc rolled half sideways and slid slowly back into the water.

I ran back to the dinghy and paddled half a mile down to the camp to get the gaff, the skinning-gear and Fiff. Back at the scene of the kill we were probing around in ten feet of water when there was a hissing snort behind us. We turned in time to see the croc's head slide back under the water. He had come up for air, badly wounded or he would have been gone from there altogether — but he was still alive.

I picked up the rifle and we sat in the dinghy waiting for him to come up again. We sat there in silence for what seemed an hour, and then the big head surfaced near the bank again. I started to raise the rifle but Fiff yelled "Look!" and he went down again.

We waited a while longer with me whispering to

Fiff to wait till I got her back to camp. Then she yelled "Look!" again and pointed behind me. I clattered round in the dinghy and there was the croc, crawling out on the bank to die. I shot him fair in the ear, and then again. Fourteen foot six and a first-grade skin.

I was so pleased that I forgot to go crook at Fiff for yelling "Look!" till we were skinning the croc, and it was too late then. So I growled at her for leaving Darcy's good sharpening-stone in the grass where it might get lost. She started slinging off about me being a big fierce joker. It was high time she was put in her place again. Much more cheek out of her and I'd clip her one, to show her who was head of the family.

Darcy was very pleased with me getting that croc.

"It is better that you nearly lost him. You would have learned nothing if your bullet had killed him at first."

That afternoon we put the net out across the river for barramundi, but most of the rubbish we caught were catfish, sawfish and sharks (right up in fresh water!).

The dogs had been lying around in the water and sniffing along the banks in the shade. We were eating under our mosquito nets to keep the flies away from our food when suddenly there was a splash and half a scream from one of the dogs we were looking after. That was the last we saw or heard of him. We ran with rifles but there was nothing to see or do about it, except hope we could get the croc that had taken him next time we were out shooting at night. We never did.

We got no crocs near the camp at all and none that even looked as though it might have recently killed a dog. I went very crook at Fiff because we'd been swimming around there on the hot afternoons. It was a chilling experience.

Fiff and I started going out on our own on nights when Darcy didn't feel like it. We got a few crocs but the biggest of them was only twelve feet.

"We have already disturbed the big blokes round here. They will have moved away or be lying very quiet."

I liked using the harpoon, even when it wasn't strictly necessary. There was something exciting and kind of primitive about it. A thrill you never get from using a rifle. I always carried the harpoon in the dinghy, even in places where the water was so shallow and the creek so narrow that it was only a nuisance.

Darcy once harpooned a croc and couldn't understand why it didn't come up for air, or struggle when he pulled on the rope. When he hauled it in he found he'd killed it stone dead. The quill had gone in between the vertebrae at the back of its neck and cut the spinal cord.

In the afternoons after crocs were skinned and food was eaten, we sometimes lay under our mosquito nets and had crocodile talks with Darcy. I was beginning to understand the man. For a long time I'd been unable to work out how a man as good at his job as Darcy could be so careless with his tools. His neglected gear lost him quite a few crocs. One day his .22 wouldn't go off; on the next, the bolt on the .303 would be glued with its own rust. The harpoon would be tangled and blunt. The spotlight would go out. It was frustrating and puzzling, till I began to realise that it was his informal way of farming the crocs in a river he was going to have to return to. A man like Darcy could do a river so thoroughly it would take the crocs a long time to recover from a hundred per cent attack. The condition of his gear was his quaint method of ensuring that there would be plenty of crocs left for breeding for next time. I think that if crocodiles became so scarce that his way of living was threatened, Darcy would most probably increase his advantage by up-grading his gear with a few drops of oil now and then a getting a roll of insulation-tape for his light, and perhaps run the file over the edge of his harpoon-quill occasionally.

But it wasn't until much later, when we were going after a maneater, that I saw what Darcy really could do when it was necessary. If a croc he really wanted could be got in any known way, he could apply the best method for the conditions as expertly as any man could do it.

In spite of all he'd told us about the mystery of crocodiles, I sometimes got the feeling that I would never acquire his shadowy, unpronounceable under-standing of them. It was the way he would go extra carefully at a place with nothing to distinguish it from hundreds of other places, and there'd be a croc there.

"Did you get one in this place once before, Darcy?"

"No," he would say, looking out across the river. "But I can smell them." But he didn't mean smell in that sense — or was I imagining things?

Some rangers came and camped on the other side of the river and Fiff paddled across and invited them over for a feed of protected pigeons — just to be sociable. They must have thought she was joking because they didn't accept her invitation. Or maybe they were very unusual rangers. We dumped the stew though, just in case.

We were running out of salt, food, and new places to hunt. It was time to go back to our base camp down the river. We had a last feed of barramundi, loaded our stuff into the big boat and the remaining four dogs into the little one and arrived back at the bottom camp three weeks and two days after we'd left it. I was really beginning to be something of a croc-shooter. Darcy and I went out twice to get some live crocs, two three-foot salties and an eighteen-inch freshy, for the bloke who'd lent us his boat. Darcy took the boat and motor down the river to Yaloginda and Fiff and I drove round with all the gear.

It was I who had to break the news to the bloke about his dog being taken by a croc. Of course it turned out to be his favourite dog, one of the best bred blue-heelers in the Gulf. Crocs always select the best ones. He was quite pleased at getting the live crocs though, and there was no animosity between us.

Darcy and I drove out to collect the blitz from the camp and brought in our bags of skins to consign to the agent in Cairns.

On the trip we'd got two hundred and sixty-four feet of crocodile, according to Fiff's diary. A good five hundred quids' worth, but we wouldn't be getting the cheque till we came back from the trip we'd planned to take round the Gulf to the Robinson River — or further, if we had time before the wet season started. Perhaps even to Arnhem Land?

We left the dingo pup with the bloke I'd bought him off because he was a bit small and sick to take on a five-hundred-mile journey. (Later when we went back there the black-fellow wanted me to buy him again. If I paid two pounds for him the first time he must be worth three pounds now because he was bigger. We left him there. He was miserable in the Landrover and we had no use for him.)

8

Around the Gulf

THERE WASN'T MUCH TIMES.
We'd left it late in the year to decide on a trip to the rivers round the Gulf and six weeks or two months was all we could expect to get in before the Wet started. We were going to leave the blitz in Yaloginda and try to carry everything in the Landrover.

Two 44-gallon drums, one for water and one for petrol. Seven bags of salt. Four bags of flour. Tobacco and supplies. All the croc-shooting gear and the little dinghy lashed to the top. It was a big load.

Out across the plain to the Gregory River crossing, then we followed an old defence road for endless miles of wandering wheel-tracks, scattered bush, bulldust, and heat. Our backs sticking to the seats and dust rising in gritty film through the holes in the cab floor.

Darcy drives, I drive, nothing changing but the gears in deep dry swamps of bulldust.

We camp. Drive on. Pass the Doomidgee Mission. Sign saying "Don't stop".

"What are they so unhospitable for, Darcy?"

"The lubras sometimes run away and come to your camp if you are close by. The missions are doing great work and half-caste children are not a help to them."

Drive on. A fence. A thick waterhole. A buffalo that runs ahead through the trees and dives sideways out of sight.

"Aren't buffaloes supposed to be dangerous and charge on sight, Darcy?"

"A buffalo is like most animals. It will run before it will fight. If you wound him or annoy him or frighten him, he will turn on you. He is very strong and his anger is great."

A herd of wild donkeys surges in a grey wave of long ears and rumps across the road ahead and vanishes in its own cloud of dust among the trees.

Camp again. Fuel up, and drive on. Shoot a big plain turkey, beautiful meat. Talk to an old man in a cool house by the road. He is caretaking for someone. (Perhaps God, who has forgotten to come back and relieve him?) He has a garden of real green vegetables and is a close friend of the musical butcher-bird and a bitter enemy of the black crow.

Drive on to Westmoreland station and pull up at a house of stones beside a fence of stones in a world of scattered stones. The countryside is changing — this is what a road would look like if we were the size of insects. Pruszkowic, a dusty host, falls weakly from the back in a shower of dust to drink noisily and endlessly at the lagoon of weeds. A sad dying pool of dirty water, crowded with small fish, in a black race-course of dry mud ploughed rough by many feet. It's been a long hot season. We are pale and coarse with dust and our hair is brittle as wire. Up to our knees in mud our waists in water. A wash in water as hot as a shower. Then a feed of salt beef and potatoes cooked by a gin at least two hundred years old.

The young station manager at Westmoreland was the only white person on the place. He was putting the finishing touches to a .303 pistol he'd cut down from an old army rifle. You often have to shoot the wild bulls in order to muster the other cattle, and galloping on a horse with a heavy rifle is an awkward business. The barrel had been hacksawed off about five inches beyond the breech and he was taping a pistol-grip on to the body of the thing. It was a dangerous-looking weapon. We were invited to witness the testing of it.

The "test-pilot" was summoned by a yell passed from one group of blacks to the other till he was located, and came shuffling up to where we were standing around being dubious and trying not to show it. He was apparently the most useful man on the place. Any horse that might buck was given to him to ride first. Any cattle that looked dangerous were tested with him. He risked his life many times a year for a couple of plugs of nikki nikki tobacco a week and his tucker, and tucker for all his family, relatives, and friends who might call in on a walkabout.

"Come here. See this rifle?"

"That one piccaninny rifle, boss!"

"It's loaded and cocked, so don't touch the trigger

till you're ready to shoot 'im. Take 'im down there and kill 'im that feller tree. Don't point it at anyone."

We got behind things while the blackfellow carried the weapon halfway down to the lagoon as though it was a sleeping taipan. There's over twenty tons of pressure in a .303 bullet when it detonates. The makers never intended them to be discharged in this manner, I'm sure. He pointed the wavering pistol at the general direction of the tree he'd been told to kill, with his arm extended and his face turned away as though from a disgusting sight. Then he fired it.

Nobody could tell where the bullet went, but the black-fellow and the pistol went in opposite directions. It was as though he'd pulled the trigger some time after he'd leapt away from it. The boss told him off for dropping the thing in the dirt. Then, seeing as how it hadn't blown up, he tried it himself. It nearly leapt out of his hand and the bullet kicked up a faint geyser of dust away out to one side.

We were all invited to have a go with the fabulous .303 pistol and we all declined. It was an ugly and cumbersome-looking piece of work. By the time we left, two hours and about thirty hair-raising explosions later, the boss had reached the stage where he could hit a four-foot-six tree trunk at six feet by holding the thing tightly in both hands. There was little likelihood of the project becoming a raging success for anything but terrifying the blacks, who were by now standing away in tight apprehensive groups.

Drive on. Country the same as the plains only rolling, with rocky ridges hunched between gullies where water has been flowing a long dry time ago. Growth in the gullies a little greener, but most of it the same dusty brown-green of a hundred miles back. And hundreds of miles beyond that.

Pass Wollogorang, right on the Queensland-Northern Territory border. Fiff says we are now best professional croc-shooters in Queensland *and* the Northern Territory.

Turn off on a scoured, bouldery track that was once a road and creep in low reduction two miles to a copper mine Darcy knows about. There's just time before dark to look around. The big blue hole and heaps of ore. The grave of the prospector who lived there for years, mining a few bags of the rich copper when he needed food or gear. The cave he lived in up on the bluff. Everything left exactly as when he was there a year before, except the bulging brown coils of a twelve-foot rock python piled on the bunk hanging on wire from the roof. Fresh, clear water up in the rocks!

Camp on snapping leaves under the big mango tree on the flat, decide not to pinch the handy little camp-oven from the cave, and take off next morning through the rocks and dust for Calvert Hills station. A glittering aluminium homestead in a sea of dirt and rocks.

Friendly people. Tidy, well-dressed black girls. Boss away but due back. Hundreds of goats. Six clean white Brahman bulls, flicking their long ears at flies by the waterhole. Imported to cross with the Hereford because they're quieter, less attractive to ticks, keep together, fight off dingoes, and don't mind the hot waterless conditions. A handful of hope for relief from the constant setbacks of disease, dingoes, and water — too much and too little.

Tie Pruszkowic to the Landrover and stay the night. Fiff and I are woken by dogs barking and shouts down by the blacks' camp in the early hours. Darcy comes panting stealthily up the outside stairs and curls up in his swag on the floor. Lonely, poor bastard.

On to Robinson River station next day with full bellies and fresh beef.

"They give us beef because they know we shall take a whole cow to salt down if they don't." (Darcy's in a bad mood this morning.)

Shoot a 'roo for Pruszkowic and give half of it to the boss at Robinson River for his dogs. Get directions and travel downstream to a long deep lagoon in the river bed. Crocs again at last. What a trip.

Forty-eight freshies in the mile-long lagoon the first night, and thirty-two the second. They were thick! Skinning and scraping, daylight to dark.

Move on down towards the sea, one walking ahead scouting a patch for the crawling Landrover. All the time shooting crocs, moving on again and shooting more crocs. Skinning crocs at waterholes, lagoons and river banks. Fiff up to her knees in the water with rifle-fish darting round her legs for floating fragments of scraped croc-meat.

Darcy taught us how to get a cool drink of water from a lagoon that is uncomfortably warm even to sit in. You take a pannikin and swim out to deep water, then dive, holding the empty mug carefully upside-down. Swim down to the cool water near the bottom of the lagoon and turn the pannikin up the right way. The air will bubble out, cool water will bubble in and you swim to the surface with your cool drink. I often wonder now why we didn't worry about crocodiles when we were doing all this swimming, but with Darcy there we didn't think of them. Perhaps he knew. In some places he would say: "We shall not swim here," and we wouldn't. Where he swam, we knew it was safe.

Fiff and I were both beginning to feel the lack of privacy in these camps. Darcy was anything but an eavesdropper. But it wasn't as simple as his just walking pointedly away from the camp for a couple of hours every now and again so we could have a talk or make love. There was need or excuse for him to do so, and we were so busy with the shooting and doing the hides that all our spare time was spent resting in the sweltering shade under mosquito nets away from the flies and the sight of croc-skins. Fiff and I would have been more alone in a city. It was so hot that even at midnight Pruszkowic lay panting outside our net as though he'd just had a hard run on a hot day. In this heat it was ridiculous for a man working as hard as Darcy was to go for walks in the afternoon sun during the only time he got to rest. So Fiff and I either spoke personal things at night in whispers or not at all.

Then one day when the skins were done Darcy said he would go on his own that night to the far end of the lagoon we were at, camp there for a few hours and shoot his way back to our camp before daylight. He wanted to see if the crocs were any different to shoot here at the end of darkness instead of at the beginning. There was no need for me to come as he was going over water we'd already covered and he wasn't expecting to get more than half a dozen or so. I was easy to convince. Fiff and I would have a whole afternoon, evening and night to ourselves!

Like hell. Darcy had been gone no more than an hour when two ringers rode up leading packhorses and stopped for a yarn and a brew of tea. They came from a station down the coast and were looking for a good yearling cattle-beast to kill for beef for the station.

"But this is Jack Earp's country," I pointed out.

"That's right," they agreed.

They hung around talking and asking about crocs, and wondering about Fiff being there, till four blackfellows came down the river on horses and joined us. They were on their way to the next station looking for a killer too. It was quite a situation. The two ringers from the place down the coast only grinned a bit and the blacks didn't show any embarrassment whatever. They were just doing what was always done.

They camped the night with us and sat round talking till all the handy wood for the fire was burnt.

So much for our night on our own.

In the morning they drew maps for each other in the dirt with sticks and explained where the best killers on each other's places were likely to be found. Then they rode away to steal beef from each other. Darcy arrived just as they were leaving. He'd been skinning a sixteen-foot salty that had given him a very exciting time. Fiff and I snarled at each other all day.

I told Darcy about the two lots of ringers going off to kill each other's beef.

"Yes," he said, "that is right. They never kill their own beef if they can help it. One man kills the other's beef because he knows the other man is killing his, but it is not talked about. The croc-shooter kills everybody's beef. They know he is doing it, but as long as he salts all the meat he cannot eat at once and doesn't waste any, that is not talked about either. A croc-shooter can save many cattle."

We only got four salties on that stretch but plenty of freshies, hundreds of them. When we'd had enough we easily found a place where the Landrover could go no further and followed the river back up to the station. We were going on to Manangoora, and perhaps right over to Borroloola, on the McArthur River.

We bellied the Landrover in loose sand and had to winch it backwards out of the river bed with a Spanish windlass we rigged up with wire, poles, rope, and sweat. Fiff was heart-broken at our 'rover having to be helped out of a hole and said it must be getting old — or tired from carrying all our things all that way. I arranged for the so-called timing-gear in the transmission-case to have slipped again, but I think she was getting a bit suspicious. Then Darcy ruined everything good and properly by asking me to explain how a timing-gear in a transmission-case worked. Fiff lost faith in me and the Landrover for days over that.

In a cool station homestead during hot cups of tea we talked about the blacks and their ways. The boss told us how his men would sometimes come and say to him: "We go now, boss." And they'd go walkabout just like that. Regardless of how much work had to be finished or done. Nothing would bribe them to stay once they'd decided to go walkabout. They'd reappear just as suddenly, weeks or months later, as though nothing had interrupted the daily routine of station life. Some of the distances they travelled on foot were incredible. There were often blacks on walkabout staying at the station and they were usually fed without question till they moved on again.

He described the fear of the house-girls when they first felt the kerosene fridge. And the antics of two of them standing on chairs trying to blow out the electric light when he'd installed a lighting plant a few years before. The stick-fights they have where people seldom get hurt — and strange incidents where some-one obviously does.

We camped that night beside the waterhole that supplied the homestead with water. Half a dozen "tame" freshwater crocs lay around on rocks and logs watching us cook steaks for dinner. In the morning we dumped our skins and the dinghy in a spare shed and then drove all day to Manangoora, on the banks of the Foelsche river. There we met an old man who was a genuine philosopher. Old Andy was wonderful to talk to, and very funny at times. He got his meth-ylated spirits in four-gallon drums and drank it with great relish. The labels had skulls and crossbones and said NOT TO BE TAKEN, and instructions about what to do if accidentally swallowed.

"But they put poison dye in that stuff," I told him.

"Rubbish," he snorted. "They wouldn't dare put

anything poisonous in metho. They'd kill off half the Northern Territory if they did that!"

We bunked down late that night under a lean-to beside his hut and woke up next morning covered with fleas and dogs and dust. Darcy and Andy were old mates and sat in the shade talking about politics and people. So Fiff and I wandered around having a look at the place and people. Andy was the only white man there and the blacks lived in a big camp across the river because of having dozens of dogs. They paddled back and forth in dug-out canoes and when Andy wanted someone he'd go out on the bank and shout at the top of his voice. They never knew who it was he wanted because of the distance and the fact that he could never remember their names, though he knew them well enough. So one of them would get into a canoe and begin to paddle over. Andy would then shout and wave him or her back, and another one would climb into the canoe and begin to paddle over — and so on till they fluked the one Andy wanted.

"Fools!" he would say, brushing spit from all the shouting into his big white beard. "The Native Affairs has taken all my good blacks away." Then he would sit in his big chair like a king to await the arrival of the summoned native.

The blacks obviously respected old Andy and took very little notice of this shouting. He ran a few head of cattle and his requirements were few and simple.

"God put me in this blasted place, and it's His job to look after me!" said Andy indignantly.

(But we'd heard rumours that he was very cop-shy about something that happened years before.)

Winston Churchill was a fossilised blackfellow, very good at making spears. He could only mis-use a few words of English but he was a sharp old bloke and he and I got to understand each other quite well after a while. I stopped to watch him binding four wire prongs on the shaft of a fish-spear with string that had been waterproofed with the black wax from the hives of the small stingless sugarbag-bees.

He never looked up or gave any sign that he knew I was standing there, but when he'd finished he began making a new spear from a twisted piece of jindy-jindy. He heated the bends in the coals of a fire he'd lit to keep the sandflies away. When the shaft was nearly bursting into flames he took it and patiently worked the bends out of it. Again and again, till the eight-foot shaft was as straight as a gun-barrel. Then he cut four slots for the prongs and fitted and bound them, bound the thin end to stop it from splitting, and dug a little hollow in the tip for the woomera to fit in. He produced a woomera with a croc-tooth bound neatly to it for a hook and expressionlessly chopped a few quick and accurate practice shots into floating leaves at the shallow edge of the river.

Then, looking at me for the first time, he handed me the spear and woomera to try for myself. In a week I was getting fish with them. The force and accuracy you can get with a good fish-spear and woomera, up to about fifteen yards, is astonishing.

I traded Winston Churchill a tin of Log Cabin tobacco for the spear and woomera. He made the exchange as though the price and value had been agreed on from the first. Then he paddled a big canoe — expertly, like Darcy — across the river and came back with two long light kangaroo-spears and a big woomera with carved flat sides. The spears were very light and whippy, with heart-shaped heads, cut from a fuel drum, bound smoothly on to them. Without taking any notice of me again he began to practise throwing the spears at an old sheet of corrugated iron he propped against a pandanus palm. He could plop one of those spears right through the sheet of iron at sixty yards. The velocity was so great and the trajectory so flat that the spear-heads cut through the tin without damaging themselves.

I was impressed. He didn't lob the spear, as I'd imagined they did. He held it level at his ear, shook it so it whipped slightly and wasn't drooping, and threw it straight as a dart. One of those coming straight at you would be very hard to dodge, or even see.

I noticed when I retrieved the spears for him the third time that one of the heads was coming a little loose, so I rummaged in the Landrover and swapped him Fiff's wristwatch for the two spears and woomera before he damaged them demonstrating. You can buy five-quid watches in any town.

After a lunch of dugong steaks and camp-oven bread, baked that morning by Fiff, I saw Winston Churchill walking around obviously with two long-bladed spears with short crooked shafts. I went out to see what this lot was and he explained with a few indecipherable words and many graphic actions that they were stabbing-spears for killing cattle. Apparently they run up beside a dozing cattle-beast, shove the spear into its ribs and nip out of the road before it realises what is happening. The spears often get broken when the beast falls, so not much trouble is taken to find straight handles for them.

I showed Winston Churchill my .222 with the 'scope and told him he could fire a shot through it. He did — right through a bark humpy down on the river bank. Thank God nobody was in it, or beyond it. Then he impassively swapped me his two cattle-killing spears for my sixty-five-quid rifle. There was an expression on his face when I took it back and exchanged it for a pocket-knife with gadgets. His not too distant ancestors wouldn't have understood at all. But he can't have borne me a grudge because he returned later with two intricately-carved and impressive-looking killing boomerangs. They were about two feet six inches long and roughly the shape of a flattened giraffe's head and neck. They aren't supposed to return once they're thrown and if one of them hits you it would be a long time before you were interested in what happened to it afterwards. I found a cartridge belt, a big silvery brooch, and a brass bangle of Fiff's to exchange for them.

I was fascinated by the balance and workmanship in the paddles they used to steer and paddle their big rough canoes. Darcy had told me how they often take days to find a suitable piece of wood — and carve a paddle to replace one that's been lost or broken. Chip-chipping philosophically away with a knife, using the hard edge of their heel for a chopping-block so the knife won't bite too deeply, till the finished article is smooth and weightless in the hand. They use a lump of wood about six feet long and twelve inches through with a hard flawless grain. With the same obstinate persistence they carve their canoes from big paperbark logs and bring them great distances to where they are to be used.

A blackfellow on walkabout is constantly on the lookout for spear shafts and canoe-trees and noting their whereabouts for later use. Darcy once bought a canoe from a blackfellow in the Roper for a sack of flour, a few pounds of sugar, and a mosquito net. The blackfellow had just brought it a hundred and fifty miles from up a river round the coast, where he'd spent ten weeks carving it out of the log.

I wasn't ambitious enough to want a canoe, though I would have liked one, but I wanted one of those paddles. So while Winston Churchill and I were in business I rummaged some more and found a ball of coloured string, a three-cell torch with flat batteries, a cigar, and a combination lock I'd forgotten the combination of. For all this he gave me my pick of seven paddles. I don't suppose the one I chose belonged to him but none of the onlookers protested. I suppose he squared it off with the owner later.

That night when Fiff and I were unrolling our swag we heard the unmistakable continuous croaking of a didgeridoo just around the corner. We went to have a look and there was Winston Churchill, sitting against the wall of the hut with the six-foot hollow instrument perched on his big toe. He was making the most of this impromptu market-day. The instrument was made from a hollow coolibah branch and stained in patterns of tan and white ochre. It looked very effective in the vague light from the hut window. He was droning a steady simple rhythm, sniffing air in through his nose every now and then without breaking the flow of sound. I'd love to know how he did it.

I had a turn and soon got the general idea. Doo-diddy, doo-diddy, doo-diddy-doo! We had to have that; Fiff was as keen as I was. So we got a lamp and rummaged again: A pair of Fiff's pants with holes. A red and yellow dress. A pair of thick socks. A sack-needle. A cigarette lighter with spare flints. A sheath-knife (it was a spare). A handful of marbles (Darcy's croc-eyes for stuffers!). A pair of sunglasses with one glass missing, and a bag of Minties stuck together. Winston Churchill was happy with that and we were happy with our new didgeridoo.

Next morning a lubra called Popeye looked very trim in Fiff's red and yellow dress. Not so Winston Churchill, who paraded disgustingly around, proudly wearing Fiff's holey old pink pants and the thick pair of socks.

We drove nearly a hundred miles that day to Borroloola, over a road deep in pools of bulldust so fine it splashed like water, with the jolting roots of trees in the holes to slow us down. At the McArthur River crossing we had to wait for two hours till the tide went out enough for us to cross. We roared across with water over the bonnet and Fiff squealing with delight (that's where all our films got soaked) and drove round to Borroloola on the other side, a couple of miles downstream.

We bought warm bottles of beer at the store, talked with people Darcy knew, and took rum and beer to visit Roger up on the hill above the river. Everybody knows old Roger at Borroloola. He lives in a square water-tank, trades things, wears half a dozen different hats, and calls himself a lotus-eater. He's got bad eyesight, long hair, and all the time in the world for interesting discussions. We talked, drank, and ate till the moon went down at midnight. Then Fiff and I spread our swag on the ground not quite out of ear-shot but so we could whisper about Roger or Darcy if we wanted to. They were still talking in rumbly voices over a bottle of overproof rum when we went to sleep.

That night someone swam across the river to the Native Affairs camp, but the dogs drove him back again.

By mid-day of the second day we'd seen all of Borroloola there was to see and there wasn't much time before the Wet was due to start. We drove back to Manangoora and arrived there in the dark and smothered in dust.

9

Goodbye to Yaloginda

WE LEFT MANANGOORA next morning and arrived at Robinson River that afternoon. We checked our skins next day for red-heat and scale-slip, used the last of our salt on some of the doubtful ones and packed them in bags on the Landrover. Six hundred and seventy-one skins and forty-six stuffers! It was a hell of a load.

The next day, Calvert Hills, and on towards Westmoreland while it was still daylight, to get a good start in the morning. We camped that night by a waterhole beside the road. A dozen or so blacks on walkabout were camped under bark humpies on the far side of the waterhole. They didn't answer when we waved out hello to them, just shyly ignored us. That was the camp where two grey and white butcher-birds came right up to us for scraps. Fiff wanted me to catch one for a pet without frightening it.

That night I broke out the didgeridoo for a bit of practice and began to drone lugubriously to the stars.

Then from the blacks' camp across the waterhole we heard sticks beating a kind of rhythm and a murmuring of voices. The murmuring voices gained volume until we couldn't possible fail to mistake what they were saying, or shut it out of our minds.

Tea-binnish, sugar-binnish, blour-binnish, bacca-binnish. Tea-binnish, sugar-binnish, blour-binnish, bacca-binnish. Tea-binnish, sugar-binnish, blour-binnish, bacca-binnish. Tea-binnish, sugar-binnish, blour-binnish, bacca-binnish teabinnish sugarbinnish blourbinnish. . . . We called one of them over for a few handfuls of our last flour and a handful of tobacco to keep them quiet for a while, a short while. They started up again an hour or so later, when we were trying to get to sleep. That cost us a tin of sugar, half a pound of tea, and another handful of tobacco.

During the night they chanted twice more and twice as loud. We were poorer in supplies and sleep when we drove away from there at daylight. And we made a rule about no one playing the didgeridoo anywhere near a blacks' camp in future, in case that was what had started them off.

That day we came to a bushfire and had to drive for about half a mile with flames leaping on both sides of the road because it was coming up behind us . Darcy and I weren't only sweating from the roasting heat in the cab of the Landrover. There was a half-full drum of petrol on the back.

Fiff said how ridiculous we were. *Our* Landrover wouldn't blow up. It was unthinkable! When we stopped in clear country the tarp we'd put over the load had enough smouldering holes to write it off. It had been a good tarp, too. We dragged it off, extinguished it, and left it on the side of the road. While Darcy and I continued sweating with relief. Fiff picked some leafy twigs off a stag-waddy bush to put in the front of the Landrover because stag-waddy was such a nice name.

Next day we left the road on a vague set of wheel-tracks and drove about ten miles to a lagoon Darcy knew about. This lagoon was over a mile long with sandy beaches round the shores and thousands of birds. Clumps of pelicans on sandbars as though they'd grown there, delicate pink flamingos strutting in slow motion along the shallows, spoonbills out on the claypan like dropped pieces of white paper. A bronze fish-eagle lying in the air and little black and white ducks wheeling and whistling in formation. There were two big cranes sitting in a dead tree with a nest in it like a log-jam. Curlews came and went and a stupid-looking frog-mouthed owl came and stayed watching. We'd never see such a collection of birds. There were some that even Darcy didn't recognise. And the lagoon itself was salt water, fifteen miles from the sea. (Darcy says it might be seepage — he's probably right.)

We camped and went out that night in the dinghy to see if we could pick up a croc or two. We shot four very easy freshies and lit up a medium-sized salty at the far end who wasn't so easy. The shooting must have alarmed him. He was out on the bank when we first spotted him. At fifty yards he slid into the water and came up about ten yards from the shore in a little bay. At thirty yards he went down and stayed there. We waited around for about twenty minutes with the light off, and then another twenty minutes with it on. When we were a couple of hundred yards on our way back down the lagoon to try for a small freshy we'd missed before, Darcy shone the light back and there was our salty. In exactly the same place. He let us get to the thirty yard mark and went down again, just as he had the first time. We waited, left, looked back, and there he was again, still in the same place. Darcy chuckled two soft chucks.

"We don't need that bloke's skin, but it would please me to get him. He is the kind of croc who will kill men and cattle when he is older. He thinks he has us beaten, but he is in error. We shall catch him with our net, and get a few pounds for the publican at Yaloginda, and perhaps save some man's cattle."

I asked him how he could tell it was going to turn into a maneater, but he said it was only an excuse to go after him.

"A maneater is better to kill than a croc that lives on crabs."

We went back to the camp, got the net and ran it out in the lagoon to straighten the loops and tangles. Then we folded it in the stern of the dinghy, cork-line on one side and lead-line on the other, and paddled back up the lagoon. Darcy gave me instructions on the way. Our croc was still there, in the same place. And he went down when we were the same distance from him as before. Only this time we didn't wait.

As soon as the eyes disappeared we paddled quickly to one end of the little bay. I had a moment of panic when I saw there was absolutely nothing to tie the end of the net to. Darcy whispered: "It doesn't matter, just begin to put it out." So I began feeding the net over the stern while he paddled out beyond where the croc had gone down, and back towards the beach in a semi-circle. We tested the depth at the furthest point from the beach very quietly with the harpoon-pole. It was just over nine feet; the net was ten.

The net was about ten yards short but Darcy just kept paddling till the dinghy beached. We pulled the boat up on the beach to anchor that end of the net. Then Darcy kept the light on his forehead sweeping the cork-line and the rifle ready, while I nipped up the beach to hold the loose end of the net. I ran into trouble.

At first I couldn't find the end of the net because it was so dark and because the end of it was ten yards out in the water. Dragging the other end in had pulled this end out. I didn't like the set-up in the least. There was supposed to be a potential maneater inside the net somewhere. I was even tempted to hope it had moved away and there'd be nothing more deadly than a fat barramundi in that black semi-circle of water attached to Darcy's head by the sweeping light. He was concentrating on the centre of the net now and hadn't seen the problem I was faced with, which was just as well — I'd wasted valuable seconds already. Darcy would have gone straight in and brought the net to the beach.

Ten yards is a hell of a long way. I swam out because I didn't care to risk the feeling of wading out of my depth. I grabbed the cork-line and swam anxiously back towards the beach, but I didn't get anywhere. It takes more horsepower than I had, even then, to drag sixty yards of heavy net through the water.

As soon as I'd begun to swim Darcy's light flicked on to me, and now he was running up the beach shouting, "Dig his eyes! Dig his eyes!"

Damn his eyes! I was still swimming desperately for the beach when Darcy waded out beside me, dragged the net up on the sand and put his foot on it — laughing. I stood up. It was waist-deep. I was glad of the darkness then. It was too late to be quiet by this time. Darcy said that when I went into the water it sounded like the twenty-footer he'd been hoping to see for years, dragging a draught-horse under. (I must have been unconsciously trying to frighten the croc away.) He put the light on the splashing and saw me apparently struggling in the water. He had to leave the light in the dinghy because he couldn't run with the lamp, and come dashing along the beach, sure that I was trying to stop the croc sneaking round the end of the net.

"But when you began to swim back I knew there was no crocodile there," he said. "It would take a football team of twenty-footers to make such a splashing." He grinned as he said it, but I still felt lousy, and there was salt water in my nose. Darcy slapped my wet shoulder with a hand like a hornback and said, "I once woke up in my canoe and fired three shots at a log that had floated against it. I didn't hit the log either. Now if you hold this end of the net I shall go and shine the light to make sure the croc doesn't go over the top of our net, if he is still with us."

I stood on the end of the net while Darcy walked

towards the dinghy end. A minute later the light raked along the curved row of corks from one end to the other.

"Begin please to pull the net from the water very slowly," called Darcy. "Don't lift the lead-line from the bottom or he may creep underneath."

I began to draw the net in. I was doubtful about the croc being inside it. Surely he would have tried to get out through it before this. There wasn't even a — hey! What's this? The net jerks in my hand. Then another double tug. Something heavy. That's no fish. It must be him! The light flicks to a swirling gap in the row of corks twenty yards from Darcy's end. The tail curls out of the water and sinks again with a jerk. We've got him.

"Give him a little time to mesh properly!" calls Darcy calmly from behind the light. "Now bring him in."

I walked along the water's edge, laying the net on the beach behind me, till I reached Darcy. Between us we pulled him ashore. The net was thoroughly tangled in his jaws — an eight-footer. One of the black ones with a yellow belly. He wasn't even resisting. Darcy shot him with the .22. Now to try and untangle the net. What a mess!

"I don't think we should worry your wife with stories of us being in the water with nets and crocodiles," said Darcy on the way back to camp. "She is a brave little woman, but it would be easy for her to misunderstand and think we were exposing ourselves to foolish dangers."

That made me feel worse, and I didn't tell Fiff about it till we were in Cairns a few weeks later.

Fiff and I woke up at the first suspicion of daylight next morning. There was something terribly wrong. The sky was bigger than the earth and plunging down on us from the north in enormous bursting rolls of blanket-grey cloud. Everything was still and impending. Not so much as a feather stirred on the lagoon, and the water was like black frozen oil.

The Wet was coming — no, a hurricane? They've dropped one of their bloody bombs in the Gulf? I burst out of the swag and mosquito net, yelled for Darcy and scrambled into the Landrover. I turned it facing the looming ruin, put it in low reduction and low gear, and pulled the handbrake on. Then Fiff and I started throwing the most valuable of our gear into the cab, cursing the fire that had burnt our tarpaulin.

Darcy started laughing behind us. He was still in his swag, grinning under the lifted corner of his mosquito net.

"What are you doing?" he asked.

"Look!" I pointed at it.

"Yes. Is very pretty, isn't it?"

"What is it?"

"A morning-glory. It will pass."

"But what the hell is it?"

"I think they start as storms out in the Gulf. They fade away over the land. It is a sign that the wet season is approaching. But there is no danger from them."

He was right. The hurricane-bomb dissolved over our heads without more than a few big drops of rain. The dawn we thought had been extinguished forever glowed in the lagoon and birds began to fly and flap and wade.

We made short work of the five croc-skins we'd got the night before, loaded up and climbed into the Landrover to set off for Yaloginda. Then I found I'd pulled the handbrake on so hard I couldn't let it off again. Both Darcy and I with our feet up on the dashboard couldn't get enough pressure to budge it. I had to crawl underneath with a spanner and loosen off the bolts.

A short-cut across to the main road to make up time turned into a fine state of confusion. Darcy said we were travelling parallel to the road in the direction of Borroloola. I thought he was wrong but didn't know where was right. Fiff said we were in a position that we could only have reached by crossing over the main road. I could have sworn the sun was off-course. We eventually came to the wheel-tracks less than a mile from the lagoon, after ploughing round in the Mitchell grass for an hour and a half.

Then the motor over-heated because the cooling system was suffocated by all the grass-seed choking the radiator. It took Darcy and me hours to clear it and cut a new gasket for the rocker-gear cover. The old one had been cooked by the excessive heat.

That afternoon we spent nearly an hour lying in the big pipes of the culvert at the Gregory River crossing, with the water trickling round us, lovely and cool, washing the dust from our eyes. Our voices echoed like dreams when we talked and Pruszkowic stirred up mud in everyone's pipe.

We covered about forty-five miles that day.

We arrived at Yaloginda too late to get any sleep and too early for the pub. So Fiff and Pruszkowic slept by the river while Darcy and I strolled across to wake up the publican.

"He knows I might be spending the wet season here," said Darcy. "He will be happy to oblige us."

The publican wasn't exactly happy, but he obliged. Stoneball Jackson was asleep in the bar, so we woke him up to help us celebrate our successful trip round the Gulf.

Fiff brought sandwiches over to the pub for us at lunchtime and joined us for a while and then went to sort out our dusty clothes to be washed.

I managed to drive the Landrover down to our old camp on the bank of the Manara River that night, but I wasn't feeling very healthy. When we pulled up there I wasn't quite being sick. Fiff unrolled our swag for me to fall on to. Darcy lumbered around in the headlights like the shadow of a bear, gathering wood, and lighting the fire. Fiff was the only one who could drink her cup of tea.

Darcy said, "A man is insane in his head. He works hard for money to buy bad health.' Then he lay down on his swag and in a few minutes was snoring like the distant bellowing of mating crocodiles. Fiff and I crawled into our swag (to hell with the bloody mosquito net). Every time I relaxed to let myself sleep my head started whirling round as though I was on the end of a stockwhip someone was cracking with all his might — and not quite wanting to be sick again. I lay awake for hours, concentrating on counting Fiff's pulse with a finger lightly on her temple.

I don't remember finally going to sleep but I certainly remember waking up next morning. Darcy and I were covered with mosquito-bites and had groaning, creaking hangovers. Fiff only had mosquito-bites. We sat with blank splitting minds and hot mugs of tea till we began to feel a little better. By that time it was two o'clock in the afternoon.

"Where are you going to spend the Wet, Darcy?" Fiff asked him.

"Here in Yaloginda," he replied. "There is nowhere else for me to go. I have no interest in the cities. Here I can be comfortable and live as I like and talk with my friends in the pub. When the rains go in March I shall shoot some more crocodiles. My money will be gone then and I shall owe many pounds to my friend the publican. He trusts me because he knows I shall always return. It is my home."

"What about us?" asked Fiff.

"You must leave the Gulf before the rains flood the roads. You would not be happy here if you couldn't leave. It's no place for a woman whose man is always at the pub. There's nothing else to do while it rains. Go to Cairns and work there till you can return and shoot crocs again."

"Good idea," I said. "We'll probably do that. We could take the croc-skins with us and post your money straight back. You'll get it a lot quicker that way. Your last cheque took a month to get here."

"On one condition you can take the skins to Cairns with you," said Darcy. "You must promise to keep your half of the money you get for them. Otherwise you can take half the skins."

"Cut it out, Darcy. You're the one who got most of them. Make it a third."

"No, half. The two of you and your truck contributed more than half. Please don't let money spoil the memory of a pleasant trip."

"Do you really want us back after the Wet?" asked Fiff.

"I would be pleased to have your company. But we should not make plans for so far ahead. If we meet again we can talk about it then." He turned to me. "You can learn more from experience than I can teach you now. You lack the patience to be a really good croc-shooter. So does nearly everyone. Such a man would be useless for anything else, and you have a woman to look after and children to breed. You will get as many crocodiles as the next man, until you become tired of it and learn another way of life."

"We'd better get away tomorrow," I said.

"Yes." That afternoon we drove Darcy and Pruszkowic in to the garage to pick up their blitz. It was like a reunion. Darcy celebrated again and Pruszkowic had his blitz to look after again. Fiff and I got an early night in, and in the morning we left Darcy still asleep and went in to Yaloginda to say goodbye and top up with fuel. We left the Landrover at the garage and walked to the pub next door for a last drink. The publican shouted us a can of beer each and everyone shook hands and drank with us. Stoneball Jackson came in just as we were leaving, gave Fiff a soft orange, and said how sorry he was about her having such a rotten bastard of a husband.

We said goodbye all round again and climbed into the Landrover. We'd gone ten yards or so on our way to Cairns when there was a long, thunderous, clanging crash behind us. It was still going when we'd stopped. An empty 44-gallon drum rolled past as I got out. There were drums all over the place. Someone had tied a long rope round the bottom tier of a pile of empty drums that were stacked beside the garage for the carrier to pick up. The other end of the rope was still tied to the 'rover. There were exactly forty-eight of those drums scattered around. Two deep, eight along, and three high. Fiff and I rolled them back and stacked them up again, while Stoneball Jackson drank innocently from a stolen can in the pub doorway.

We stopped at the camp by the river to say goodbye to Darcy and Pruszkowic and put a few last things in the Landrover. Darcy helped us fix the load and then we rolled smokes from a tin of Log Cabin, wondering what to say.

"Write a letter to me care of the pub," said Darcy. "You are just ahead of the first rain." We all looked up at the sky. The sun was already losing the sting of summer, smouldering sullenly behind the clenched clouds of the rival season. Darcy was right. I glanced at him.

He was a lonely man, no matter how much company there was. I had the feeling he would enjoy the solitude of working the rivers alone no more or less than when we were with him. We left him standing with Pruszkowic beside their jumbled blitz and drove away. Darcy's last wave dissolved in the swelling flourish of grey dust that spread out behind our bouncing 'rover.

Fiff and I felt very sad at parting with Darcy. He had become our closest friend.

10

A Dinghy Like Darcy's

AFTER THE WITHERING, TOASTED PLAINS of the Gulf the sudden crisp green of the countryside around Cairns was like a strange country to Fiff and me. The taste of clean cold water took a bit of getting used to, we'd been so long on brackish, muddy, and rusty hot water in the Gulf lagoons and rivers. We drove through the town and then out to some bush at the foot of the hills and camped. I think we needed a little breather to get used to all the extravagant luxury of the countryside. The dusty scruffiness of our brave Landrover looked as foreign there as we must have. So we kept to ourselves for a few hours, like new kids at school. Next morning, in our best clothes and looking as though we'd just walked over from Alice Springs, we took our croc-skins in to town and found the agent. I left Fiff sitting in the Landrover and strolled into the office rolling a smoke.

"Yes, what can I do for you?" said the bloke behind the bar.

"Got one or two croc-skins," I told him, lighting my smoke and flicking the match out the door.

"What are they?" he asked.

"Bit of everything," I said. "What are you paying?"

"Best prices you'll get anywhere. Sixteen bob an inch for first-grade saltwater bellies, eight and six an inch for freshies. How many have you got?"

"Few hundred," I said vaguely, reaching over to use his ashtray.

I backed the overloaded Landrover into the yard behind the office and Fiff and I passed out all our bags of skins. He and his two mates were quite impressed.

"Where did you get these?" one of them asked.

"Round the Gulf," I said non-commitally.

It took hours for them to unroll and measure all the skins. People came and went, having a look and asking questions. Fiff and I leaned on the Landrover looking bored. At last the boss came over with pages of figures to tell us they'd finished measuring the skins.

"Six hundred and seventy-six, I make it," he said. "Does that tally with your figures?"

I nodded carelessly. "Near enough."

He read out the number of salties, freshies, bellies, and hornbacks.

"A good line of skins," he said. "I had to second-grade seven of the ones with holes in them, but in a lot like that we usually get about five per cent of second grades. Now if you'll just come into the office

I'll work out what we have to pay you and give you a cheque."

It took him another hour to find out from his pages of figures how much to write the cheque out for.

"Two thousand seven hundred and fifteen pounds twelve and six. Who shall I make the cheque out to?"

Fiff and I were dumbfounded. We'd expected to get a few hundred quid, but not thousands.

"What name?" he repeated.

I thought quickly and could see a lot of income tax coming our way.

"Harvey Wilson," I said. It came into my head, just like that.

We took the cheque and put it in the bank, feeling that we'd struck Tatts with a ticket we didn't know we had. We posted a cheque for one thousand five hundred quid, plus a bit for exchange, to Darcy care of the Yaloginda pub, wondering whether he would remotely share our feelings about so much money — but we knew that a thousand quid either way would mean nothing to him.

Then we went out to buy ourselves clothes and gear. That night we booked into a flash pub with the critical authority of all wealthy people. We stayed long enough, one night, to discover that there were pubs and pubs — ours was the kind at Yaloginda.

So we moved into a bach behind the house of the old girl we were renting it from. She was a bit of a beaut. She went crook at first about all the old and greasy vehicle parts on her lawn and I had to do a bit of talking-round on her. Fiff and she got on okay but I reckoned she was nuts. Every time Fiff let herself get talked into going over to her house for a cup of tea she'd come back with another yarn of some crazy quirk the old girl had.

First it was about her keeping the window open whenever she had the radio on so all the used-up noises could get out of the room. Then it was about power and telephone lines. They were hollow, with light and heat and voices being poured in at the other end. Then there was the one about windows wearing thin with too much cleaning. Fiff told me off for laughing, but who could help it.

It wasn't hard to keep on the right side of the old dear, though, and she was well-meaning in a kind of impossible way. Like the time she invited us to buy a dog so she could give us all her scraps to feed it with.

The rains began and there was nothing to do but settle down to wait till March, when we could go back to the Gulf and be croc-shooters again. One of the first things I did was to give the Landrover a complete overhaul, expense no object. I fitted free-wheeling hubs to the front wheels for less wear and more miles to the gallon. New tyres all round. Ground the valves, and replaced everything I could find that was worn or wearing. That took three weeks. Then we looked around for a dinghy like Darcy's, couldn't find one for sale and eventually went to a boatbuilder and told him what we wanted. Yes, he would make us any kind of dinghy we wanted.

"Bondwood, spoon-bottom with a shallow keel? No trouble! Yes, sure you can watch me build it. You can help build it if you like."

Poor man, we must have driven him nearly frantic. Fiff would say that Darcy's boat had this and I'd say it didn't, it had that. The middle seat was further forward. No, it was further back. It had rowlocks. It did not! It was this shape. Rubbish, it was much narrower.

The boatbuilder said Darcy's dinghy must have defied all the principles of structure and shape. In the end we all compromised and the finished article was quite pleasing. It had a special place to tie the harpoon-rope, a gap in the front seat to stick the knife and a slot in the stern corner to hold the harpoon-pole from falling overboard. Fiff made me sign a paper saying I was to leave buying the paint for it entirely to her, with the usual ineffective penalty for breaking the agreement. Cumberland-stone inside, and battleship-grey on the outside. She wanted to paint *Queen of the Gulf* in black letters on each side, but I clouted down on that. (A man's got to draw the line somewhere, agreement or not.)

We drew forty quid of our crocodile money out of the bank to pay the boatbuilder in advance and cheer him up a bit. Fiff wanted to carry the money in case I lost it. She put the roll on some magazines on a shop counter while she paid for a tin of tobacco. By the time we got back to the shop it was too late. They'd never seen us before. It's just as well for her I was in a good mood. I called her a dozy old bitch and saved it up for a pub-excuse later on. So our dinghy cost us seventy-five quid instead of thirty-five — plus two pound ten for paint. It was to pay for itself many times over.

We had two harpoon-quills made, scrounged in the hills for a perfect pole, and generally fussed with our croc-gear till there was nothing else we could do with it except leave it alone. We had worn out our road map of the Gulf, so we bought a big one to pin on the wall. We marked off all the rivers from the Leichhardt to Cape York. We'd decided to shoot on our own so we could be independent, and so that he could be, too.

The Wet dragged on. I put up a fence for a cane-farmer to fill in time, while Fiff did twenty stuffers we had packed away in salt. She made a pretty fair job of them, too, and sold them all to a shop in Cairns for three bob an inch. Got nearly fifty quid for them.

Slightly before it was really sensible we took off for the Gulf again, with all our immaculate new gear in our completely done-up 'rover. Low overlapping cloud was still trailing smudgy rain through the hills and the rivers ran muddy and deep. We had to wait three weeks in a boggy camp on the banks of the Leichhardt before we got a night on the river. We never saw a croc and there was another flood after that. It was five weeks after we left Cairns when we started getting the odd croc. But nobody could say we were late getting started.

We had selected the rivers in the eastern Gulf from the Leichhardt round to Cape York Peninsula so as not to overlap into Darcy's country.

Shooting on our own we soon found that he hadn't taught us everything about croc-shooting by a long shot. We made the most ridiculous mistakes for professional croc-shooters. Things that Darcy had automatically allowed for or provided against, things he took so much for granted he never thought of telling or showing us.

We got trapped up a narrow creek by the falling

tide one evening, waiting for dark, and had to wait four and a half hours for enough water to float us out to the river again. The mosquitoes nearly killed us.

Then, a week or so later, we went up an overgrown waterway at low rising water and waited for dark. It was a spring tide that floated our dinghy up among the overhanging branches, until we had to hack and drag the boat out through the trees to the main river. A hell of a business.

One night in Saxby we were going round collecting stuffers because there were no big crocs about. I drifted the dinghy under an overhanging tree, where we'd spotted a little flash of red eyes, and I leaned over the bow to grab the stuffer. I was less then three feet away and still closing in when I saw it was a thirteen-foot salty with leaves blotting his eyes. I damn-near screamed. The croc sloshed backwards and disappeared just before we ran into him. He came up in the middle of the stream a few minutes later and I paddled carefully across and shot him very hard in the head for scaring me like that.

We also made mistakes Darcy had warned us about. ("You will know these things, but you will not have learned them till you are taught by experience.")

There was the time a dead nine-foot salty suddenly came alive in the bottom of the dinghy, its head thrashing around between Fiff's feet. He couldn't get his nose out from under the seat, fortunately, but I couldn't use the axe on him because of the risk of holing the boat. We very nearly capsized. I shot him in the head and hoped the bullet wouldn't go right through, but it did. We patched the hole and always made thorough use of the axe after that.

We lost a bag of skins through being skimpy with the salt and another through not checking and resalting them. We lost out on a lot of crocs while we were learning the rivers, but we made a comfortable amount of money all the same. We wandered from river to river till we got to know each one. Then we went on wandering from one to another. The Leichhardt — the Saxby and the Flinders — the Norman — the Gilbert – the Mitchell, and all the little side creeks and lagoons we could ransack with our light for the red eyes of crocodiles.

One morning Fiff says we should go to the Gilbert because we can pick up fresh bread on the way. I rubbish the idea for being stupid, but later that morning I tell her to start loading up. We're heading for the Gilbert so I can get some more tobacco at Normanton because all the Log Cabin is in a box underneath the stuff I've already put in the 'rover.

We met quite a few more best professional croc-shooters in Queensland and/or the Northern Territory, but none of them were getting any more crocs than we were. Most of them a lot less. Some of them were as Australian as a quartpot, born and bred with an outboard motor in one hand and a rifle in the other. Some were New Australian as crocodily as bones on a murky deep bend of a river. But none of them could have held a candle to Darcy, us included.

Our reputation as professional croc-shooters was a bit extra because of one of us being a woman, and quite a lot of people wanted to come with us on trips. Some offered big money. But we were happy the way we were, and only ever took one bloke out with us. And that was only because he was so melodramatic about everything and Fiff liked listening to him talk. He just lasted the one shortened trip.

He had a good sense of humour and we got on quite well with one half of his split-personality — the half that talked. The half that was rumoured to swing the best scraping-arm in the Gulf was almost dormant. One day I went crook at Fiff about a loaf of bread she'd burnt, and then I had to go crook at Cyril for going crook about it too. (A man's got to draw the line somewhere.)

I don't know whose idea it was, but one day we were suddenly on our way to Yaloginda to see if we were going to run into Darcy and show him that we were genuine professional croc-shooters making a lot of money.

The blitz was parked beside the Yaloginda pub as though it had never left there. Pruszkowic came to wave his tail casually at us as though we'd never left there either. We hurried into the bar and there was Darcy. Exactly the same. The only one missing was Stoneball Jackson, who was away prospecting in the Kimberleys. Darcy was more pleased to see us than anybody. He shook my hand and poked Fiff in the stomach and asked where all the babies were.

He smiled at our stories of great achievement and frowned and nodded at all the right places. We drank again from cans and talked endlessly about crocodiles. Darcy had been shooting the same rivers and getting the same kind of tallies. He hadn't got his twenty-footer yet, he told us sadly, only four more eighteen-footers. We camped that night at our old place on the Manara River.

"Come with me to the Cleland River near Seven Emus. There is a crocodile there that will teach us both something. He has been living on the blacks' dogs and the station cattle for many months, and now he is getting very cheeky. They are afraid for their children and lubras, who must go to the river to wash and swim. One man has already tried to kill him, but the croc was too cunning for him. I would like to try."

"Have a lot of crocs moved in there since, Darcy?"

"No. There are still many freshies around the Gulf there, but very few big blokes are left. And where there are few of them you learn the tricks. You will see how little I and experience have taught you about crocodiles."

11

With Darcy Again

S O WE LOADED everything we were likely to need, and a few things we weren't, on to the Landrover and took off for the Cleland River, a two-day trip. It was good to be with Darcy and Pruszkowic again. On the way Darcy told us about a trip he'd made to Sydney a couple of months before in half a dozen perfunctory statements; then he told us how he'd got caught by a flood in the Wearyan River last Wet. He was coming down with the river with about two feet of fresh floodwater in it and his loaded dinghy had been swept against a big log that had fallen right across the river. He'd had to unload all his gear and skins and pile everything on the log. Then he sank the dinghy, floated it under the log, bailed it out and loaded up again on the other side. The tree roots were going to break loose from the bank any moment and he just got clear in time.

"I was fortunate," he said calmly. "The tree followed me two miles down the river and I had to

177

paddle hard to get far enough ahead to have time to drag my boat clear of the water so it could go past."

"What's the story about this maneating crocodile in the Cleland, Darcy?"

"We shall not know that until we get there," he replied. "These stories alter with every mile they travel. They say it is the same crocodile that took a blackfellow from his canoe in the Wearyan, fifty miles away, last year. And attacked the camp of a croc-shooter in the mouth of the Cleland some months ago and took his dog. A crocodile often gets blamed for every attack in the Gulf if he is big enough and causes enough trouble."

"Do you think we'll get him, Darcy?"

"If we are lucky and he is still there. He may be gone from there when we reach the Cleland."

He wasn't. The place was in a panic. Only the day before the croc had overturned a canoe and attacked a lubra who was in it. She escaped to the river bank with only bruises on her arms and hands from beating at the croc's head. It was something of a miracle but there was no rejoicing.

The blacks' camp was a big one, half of it on each side of the river, for some reason, and they paddled back and forth in big heavy dug-out canoes.

It seemed that the croc — anything from fifteen to thirty feet long, according to who you were listening to — had appeared in the river there about two months before. The first hint of its presence were the screams of a lubra, who saw it going down the bank in broad daylight one afternoon with a frying-pan in its mouth. Next day it took a swimming dog a hundred yards up the river from the camp. And a few days later a freshly-killed calf floated up and down on the tides past the camp.

The blacks depended on the river for most of their food and the situation was becoming desperate. Their expeditions to the mouth of the river, fishing and hunting the big sea-cow, or dugong, were suspended when a young boy was dragged screaming into the river where he'd been paddling along in the shallows spearing mud-crabs.

There were about forty or fifty dogs starving noisily around the camp, but the croc wasn't. Every few days another of them disappeared into the river.

A passing croc-shooter called Richards had been persuaded to have a try at getting the croc, but while he was out hunting for signs of him another dog vanished in a howling welter of foam in the river right outside the camp. Eventually this bloke Richards had a shot at the croc at long range in the spotlight. After that the attacks had ceased and it was thought the croc had either been killed or wounded, or at least frightened away.

But now he was back in business again.

"Do you think it's the same croc, Darcy?"

"In this place it is most likely."

We set up a camp some distance from the blacks' camp and dogs and sorted out our gear. Darcy, whose reputation as the best croc-shooter in the Gulf was known far and wide, was looked to for relief from the maneater that had come to beset the Cleland River blacks. And there was a new eagerness in his manner. An authority that only seemed to flourish in the atmosphere of swamps and dark smelly places. An atmosphere of guiltless slaughter and revenge in over-hanging silences on bends of rivers. When he wasn't talking or shooting crocodiles Darcy was almost non-descript, but when there was croc in the air he was as colourful as a new scarf.

He sorted out three of the most intelligible blacks and asked questions that seemed obscure, until later, and said he'd see what he could do tomorrow about "this cheeky crocodile".

In the morning Darcy took our pick of the fifteen or sixteen canoes lined up at the bank for us. He chose one of the smallest. We checked the croc-gear carefully and Darcy put a few drops of oil on his .303 bolt from the dipstick of the Landrover.

"Will he be a big old rogue Darcy? Hundreds of years old?"

"As long as he is a big bloke it does not mean that he is very old. Age and size do not have to go together. A young man can be big and an old man can be small. You get a big pig and a small pig the same age. You can get a big dog and a small dog from the same litter of pups. Horses are big and horses are small. Why should it be any different about croco-diles? I think this might be an old-man crocodile because he let the little girl escape from him. But we shall not know until we have him dead. This man Richards has disturbed him. He will not be easy to get."

We went downstream first for a look around, Darcy in the front of the canoe and me with my new paddle at the stern. I practised paddling and steered the canoe very quietly. I'd never used a canoe before. Once we got it moving through the water its own weight carried it along with very little effort on the paddles, but it was also hard to stop and steer. Still, we only needed one chance, but we'd be lucky to get that. We went about two miles down the river, crossing over and back to peek among reeds and backwaters and examine mudbanks and beaches. On the way back to the camp Darcy surprised me by saying: "There are two small crocs living where we have looked, but it's weeks since our big bloke has lived down here."

I had seen nothing.

After lunch we went upstream. At the second bend I saw Darcy stiffen on the paddle but our momentum was too great for us to stop in time. We drifted into full view of a big black croc, curved in a great two-ton heap on a beach three hundred yards ahead. It gave me the shivers. I began to back paddle but Darcy said quietly: "We are too late. He will be watching us. Turn the canoe, and so that I'm out of his line of sight make sure he can see you all the time and can't see me leave. If he cannot see us at all he will go straight into the water. Keep his attention and I shall try to sneak up to him."

As soon as he was out of sight of the croc Darcy slipped over the side of the canoe with the .303 and swam ashore. He gently shook the water out of that long-suffering rifle and drifted into the trees on the bank. I manoeuvred the canoe around on the bend, just in the view of the motionless croc, and long enough for Darcy to have sneaked up on him twenty times over. Then I saw him, head and shoulders moving almost imperceptibly towards where the croc lay at the foot of the bank; he had been in my view for thirty yards. I'd been watching for him and hadn't seen him. He was still fifteen yards from where he would be able to look down at the croc, or the croc up at him. There wasn't a breath of wind and I'll swear not a whisper of sound or vibration of Darcy's ghostly approach, but the croc lunged indifferently into the water and sank from sight, so completely that it was hard to believe he'd ever been there on the empty beach.

Darcy took several minutes to cover the remaining distance and look down to where the croc had been, with the rifle half-raised in his hands. Then he opened the bolt and jumped down the bank to examine the marks, while I paddled the canoe along to pick him up. He didn't seem to be as disappointed as I'd expected when I got there.

"Sixteen or seventeen feet," he said, pointing with his foot to some invisible marks on the hard parched sand. "He is very big and probably very old. We shall not get him that easily."

"But how did he know you were sneaking up on him? You were nearly there. Did you accidentally make a noise or something?"

"No," said Darcy. "I made no noise. But that crocodile has rested on river banks like this one since before croc-shooters and cattle came to this country, with nothing to do but listen. It could be that the absence of sounds warned him. Insects in the grass or the ground may have grown quiet or raised tiny alarms ahead of me. We have no way of knowing that he didn't simply get tired of watching you in the canoe, or become disturbed, or just felt like a swim, or went off to search for another dog."

"Then we can never get him," I said, depressed at the thought of the croc detecting Darcy's less than audible sneaking.

"Don't be so melancholy," Darcy laughed. "While he is watching for us to sneak up to him on the bank we shall be approaching from another direction. There are many ways to kill a croc. The more he defeats us the bolder he will be. He has tasted the easy food of the dogs here, and now he watches the river for more. If he was going to leave here he would have gone when the man Richards fired a bullet at him. He is hungry now. His need for food will make him careless and give us other chances to try and kill him."

That night we tried the spotlight and lit his eyes up from the same corner we'd seen him from that day. He was out in the stream, twenty yards off the beach where Darcy stalked him. He watched till we were within a hundred yards, then turned round once, went down and stayed there for the two hours we watched. My favourite hope was gone. Darcy admitted that we were unlikely to get him with the spotlight. But he was still optimistic.

"We have only tried the two usual ways," he said. "Our croc has survived many such attempts. It is another kind of trap he will fall into — his own stomach."

That night Darcy hung a kerosene lamp on a branch at the bend of the river where we'd seen him both times.

"Just to confuse him and make him uneasy there. I do not want him in that part of the river."

Next morning we sent two parties of blacks out hunting. One to a flying-fox colony up the river and one after wallabies.

"Try to bring me a dead dingo," he said. "You can carry him in your hands because he is a dog and dogs are supposed to smell of human. But carry the flying-foxes and wallabies on a spear."

He told the blacks to keep their dogs out of the river but tie a few round the banks to remind the croc of his hunger. Pruszkowic didn't need telling or tying up.

I went out and fluked a meandering dingo with a shot at three hundred yards. The hunting parties returned with four flying-foxes and another dingo, but no wallabies. Darcy was pleased.

"That is good. I was afraid we might have to sacrifice one of the dogs. It doesn't matter now about the wallabies."

I hated handling the dead dingoes. Darcy had got a little quick-lime and a little strychnine from a bloke at Yaloginda. We put both poisons in one of the dingo-carcasses and threw it out of the canoe in a hard-to-find place in a shallow back-water.

"Make it difficult for him. If I found a meal of barramundi and hens' eggs in the middle of my table I would be suspicious. I do not like to poison a crocodile. It is not my way of killing him. But if a crocodile could do it he would take lives that way. I have set a snare and two hooks further down. We will go and bait them with the dingo and the flying-foxes."

The snare was a simple affair of thin wire rope he'd got from the winch on the front of the Landrover, but so cleverly spliced and snugly set among the mangrove roots that he had to point it out to me from four feet away. He waded through the mud with the bait and weaved it into a tangle of mangrove roots beyond the snare.

"If he starts pulling at that he will be well through the snare and his movement will dislodge it to fall round himself. A trip-weight on a snare is hard to conceal and causes you to leave too much evidence of yourself there. Simplicity can succeed where complication outwits itself. Now we'll go and bait the hooks I have set."

The hooks were ordinary shark hooks, one the gaff off the harpoon-pole and the other a spare we carried in the croc-box, with six or eight-foot lengths of the wire cable securing them to trees at the high-water mark. They were half a mile apart on the same side of the river. The first was above the water in the tree and the other laid out across the mud with the cable buried. Darcy covered his hands in mud and threaded a flying-fox on to each of the hooks. The other two 'foxes we threw out in the river as teasers on our way back to the camp.

Next morning I couldn't get Darcy into the canoe quick enough. In my haste to find out if we'd caught the croc I almost forgot to put the rifle in. The poisoned dingo was undisturbed, so was the snare, so was the first baited hook — and the second. We even found one of the flying-foxes we'd left floating in the river, still floating in the river. But for Darcy's cheerfulness I would have been very cheerless at what I saw as a complete failure. The croc could even be miles away by this time.

"It is fortunate that none of our traps were sprung

by small crocs," he observed. 'It often happens."

The day passed dull and hot. Darcy told the blacks to let all their dogs go, and they accepted this as an admission of failure. He didn't seem to mind.

Next morning it was lying motionless in the mud at the foot of the tree. The hook was caught, but only just, in the side of his mouth. Near the hinge by the look of it. The wire strand was as thin as a hair-ribbon — surely he could tear the tree out by the roots with one flick of his enormous neck? Snap that wisp of wire? Straighten the hook?

Darcy steered the canoe straight down the river without a sign that he'd even seen the croc. We drew level. I wasn't putting very much weight into the paddle. Just as it looked as though we were going right on past, Darcy picked up his rusty .303 and shot it fair behind the ear. The massive tail flicked once, almost casually, sloshing mud all over us and the branches around. That was all. Except for the axe, to make really certain.

We got out and stood there in the mud beside him, just looking. Eighteen feet of him. A couple of tons at least. Broken-toothed and old — a hundred years old. Evading the blackfellow's harpoon, and the lights and rifles of croc-shooters for the best part of a century. Ranging thousands of miles of coast and river. Maybe even a trip to New Guinea now and again. By luck and cunning he'd survived for that great lifetime to end up on a hook and line, caught like a sprat. Or perhaps it was old age that had caught him? He might have been ready to die anyway.

"Why didn't he pull the hook straight, or break the wire, Darcy?"

"Once he feels himself caught he gives up," replied Darcy. "This bloke probably could have broken free. That is why we had to let him think we were going past, so we could get close enough to be sure of putting a bullet in the right place."

We stood looking some more and then Darcy said: "He knew he shouldn't have touched it. For a croc that size a flying-fox would be less than one peanut to a starving man. His stomach was empty and his brain was old and tired from listening and watching. We are lucky he didn't get food from somewhere else. We would have had to use other methods then."

"Other methods?"

"Yes. There's a trick with a net using the rise and fall of the tides I'll show you one day [he never did] and a gate-trap I learned to make on the Limmen. There are ways. Some of them sound so unlogical that they are seldom used, but they can catch crocodiles."

The shot had been heard up at the camp and canoes came belting down the river, crowded with babbling blacks. Word was shouted back up the river from canoe to canoe and more and more excited blacks came racing down to see. Men, women and children.

"We could have got a shot at him from the bank with the spotlight if we'd waited at the right place," continued Darcy, "but if we had killed him we could never have recovered him from the deep current there. And I wanted his hide. This way it is much better."

Fiff arrived among the crowding, colliding canoes of deafening blacks in a rickety old canoe with a big split down the side. Children plunged in the water and stirred up the mud in squealing delight. It was safe to swim in their river again, for the time being. Darcy was regarded with all the wonder and respect of a Messiah. We stood a little proudly by the dead croc, rolling smokes.

I heard Fiff saying "Bloody joker" and "Lizard-skinners" among the noise. I pretended not to hear, and stood critically watching four blackfellows, who'd worked for a croc-shooter the season before, begin skinning the croc. It took about fifteen of them to roll the carcass over in the mud. There would be feasting at the camp tonight, and word of this would soon be spreading from one end of the Gulf to the other.

Fiff, Darcy and I paddled back to the camp in the biggest canoe, to sit in the shade making casual remarks about "big blokes".

"But I shall never kill a twenty-foot crocodile," said Darcy sadly.

We went back to Yaloginda. Darcy stayed on there. Fiff and I went back to our eastern end of the Gulf, leaving Darcy contentedly alone in the world of snakes and rivers, trembling mirages and thirst, floods and cyclones, old-man crocodiles and sudden exploding death on the end of that rusty .303. He was returning to the Roper River to fill in the two months till the Wet started.

The season passed steadily for Fiff and me. Bumpy tracks, smoky camps, black spotlit nights, and bags of skins consigned to Cairns, and any day "Harvey

Wilson" walked in he was due for a shock from the income tax people.

We'd done what we set out to do and now we'd reached the stage where each croc we shot was reminiscent of another. As the Wet drew closer we began to wonder where we'd go next and what we'd be doing. I first noticed it when Fiff said one day, "I wonder if we're going to be pioneers, in a wild place where I'll have to do the cooking in a big open fireplace till you get the house finished? We might even have a baby?" No comment.

12

Most of the Time

ONE OF OUR FAVOURITE lying-in-bed games is remembering Darcy and the things that happened in the Gulf when we were professional croc-shooters — best professional croc-shooters. Pruszkowic twitches dreaming at our feet and raises his head and thumps his tail whenever his name, or Darcy's, is mentioned.

"Remember him putting off getting away from the pub?" Fiff will say.

"And cranking the blitz to save the battery?" I will say.

"When he first went to the Gulf he had to learn on his own. There was no one to teach him."

"With two Holden bonnets welded together for a boat."

"Looking for important things lost on the back of the blitz."

"I wonder what Pruszkowic means?"

"You're not supposed to have Alsatian dogs in the

191

Northern Territory in case they breed with the dingoes."

"Cooking the damper on a piece of green gum-bark so we won't disturb the load getting the camp-oven out of the waggon."

But we always stop short. Before the end of the story.

Pruszkowic arriving, alone, at the mission station. The search. The blitz, found forlorn, among Darcy's usual scattered camp paraphernalia. The dinghy, floating in the reeds two miles upstream, moored by the harpoon-rope trailing overboard. The .22 on the floorboards. No sign of the .303. No sign of Darcy.

He told me once, "You are not to be blaming the crocodile for every death on the river. But most of the time it is he."

Perhaps he had found his twenty-footer.